Megan Tschannen-Moran

Trust Matters

Leadership for Successful Schools

JOSSEY-BASS
A Wiley Imprint
www.josseybass.com

Published by Jossey-Bass
A Wiley Imprint
989 Market Street, San Francisco, CA 94103-1741   www.josseybass.com

Jossey-Bass books and products are available through most bookstores. To contact Jossey-Bass directly call our Customer Care Department within the U.S. at 800-956-7739, outside the U.S. at 317-572-3986 or fax 317-572-4002.

Jossey-Bass also publishes its books in a variety of electronic formats. Some content that appears in print may not be available in electronic books.

Library of Congress Cataloging-in-Publication Data
Tschannen-Moran, Megan, date.
  Trust matters : leadership for successful schools / Megan
Tschannen-Moran.—1st ed.
     p. cm.
  Includes bibliographical references and index.
  ISBN 0-7879-7434-X (alk. paper)
  1. School supervision—United States—Case studies. 2. Teacher-principal
relationships—United States—Case studies. 3. Educational
leadership—United States—Case studies. I. Title.
  LB2806.4.T77 2004
  371.2'00973—dc22   2004002653

Printed in the United States of America
FIRST EDITION
HB Printing   10 9 8 7 6 5 4 3 2 1

Contents

Tables, Figures, and Exhibits

For Bob, Bryn, and Evan
From whom I have learned the
most important lessons about trust

Preface

Once on a record-breaking cold Chicago morning, my husband, then a young inner-city pastor, got a call from a disabled church member saying that she would like to go to church. Being both kind-hearted and bull-headed, he was determined to get her there despite the obstacles. He had to borrow a car, start it, and warm it up in subzero temperatures. With persistence, he was able to get the car started and running. Presently, however, the engine light came on and the smell of smoke ignited an alarming realization: the oil was frozen in the oil pan. Without lubrication, the engine over-heated and died—entailing a costly repair to replace the engine. This incident provides an apt metaphor for what it is like to try to run a school without trust. Trust functions as a lubricant of organizational functioning; without it, the school is likely to experience the overheated friction of conflict as well as a lack of progress toward its admirable goals.

Schools once enjoyed the implicit trust of their communities, and school leaders felt they could take for granted the trust of their internal and external constituencies. School leadership was by and large a high-status, low-stress job. Now, too often, it is the reverse. We live in an era in which all of our social institutions have come under unprecedented scrutiny. This trend away from trust poses a special challenge for school leaders because trust is so vital for schools to fulfill their fundamental mission of educating students to be productive citizens. Yet trust seems ever more difficult to achieve and maintain in the complex and rapidly changing world of the twenty-first century. In such a climate, understanding the nature and meaning of trust in schools has taken on added urgency and importance. School leaders need to better understand the dynamics of trust in order to reap its benefits for greater student achievement, as well as improved organizational adaptability and productivity.

Without trust, it is unlikely that schools can be successful in their efforts to improve. Nevertheless, the systematic study of trust in schools has been neglected. This book begins to fill that void. Although there is a burgeoning literature of trust outside the field of education, few educational scholars have mined this literature in order to understand the nature, meaning, and consequences of trust as it pertains specifically to the context of schools. This book brings to bear an extensive review of the literature across the social sciences to relationships of trust within schools, tapping both theoretical and empirical research spanning the past four decades. It also draws upon my own original research in over three hundred elementary and secondary schools.

This book offers practical, hands-on advice to educators on how to establish and maintain trust, as well as how to repair trust that has been damaged. The book centers around the case studies of three principals, one who has succeeded in cultivating the trust of her faculty and two who, although well-intentioned, have been unsuccessful in harnessing the vital resource of trust and whose schools are suffering impaired effectiveness as a result. It also explores the role of the school leader in fostering trust relationships among teachers, students, and parents. Although the names used are pseudonyms, the cases are based on real principals and interviews from teachers within their schools. All three led elementary schools with populations of primarily low-income and minority students within a few miles of each other in the same urban school district. But the similarities ended there. These cases provide vivid examples of how even well-meaning individuals can end up engendering the distrust of their faculty and the high cost to be paid when this happens. They also help illustrate the contrasting productivity of a high-trust school.

Chapter One explores why trust matters in schools. This chapter introduces the three principals. Gloria Davies is an overzealous reformer who has alienated her faculty and is engaged in an intense power struggle. Fred Martin, the "keep-the-peace principal," has lost the faith of his faculty by avoiding conflict. The resulting culture of distrust has a negative effect on his school's effectiveness. Gloria and Fred evidence, respectively, the "fight" and "flight" responses to conflict. These two cases are contrasted with the story of Brenda Thompson, a "high-support, high-challenge principal," who through caring and hard work has earned the trust of her faculty. Whereas Gloria took too much responsibility for the task of school improvement and Fred took too little, Brenda successfully balanced a concern for task with a concern for relationships within her school. Because changes in the social and political environment of schools have transformed the context for building trust in schools, school leaders need to be more attentive and exercise wisdom in issues of trust.

Although people generally have an intuitive understanding of what is meant by trust and have some basis on which they make trust judgments of others, trying to articulate a precise definition of trust is not easy. Chapter Two provides a comprehensive definition of trust as one's willingness to be vulnerable to another based on the confidence that the other is benevolent, honest, open, reliable, and competent. Each of these facets is illustrated with stories about Brenda Thompson, who led Brookside Elementary, a school with a high level of trust in the principal and high trust among the faculty. Brenda demonstrated proficiency in all five facets of trust. She extended care to her faculty in a variety of ways, was respected as a person of high integrity and commitment, avoided hidden agendas, worked hard, and distinguished herself as an educational leader. These attributes enabled Brenda to evoke an extra measure of effort from her teachers. Her trustworthy leadership was rewarded with above-average performance from Brookside students in measures of student achievement.

Trust is a complex and dynamic process. Chapter Three explores factors that influence the development of trust. The dynamics of initiating trust include such factors as institutional supports to fostering trust and the role that reputation plays. The role of personal factors such as the disposition to trust, values and attitudes, as well as moods and emotions are also explored. Authentic trust is the goal of this development process.

Chapter Four explores the dynamics of betrayal—what happens to provoke betrayal in a previously trusting relationship. This is illustrated by the story of Fred Martin, a well-meaning and affable principal. Fred's unwillingness to make hard decisions or to hold teachers accountable resulted in his faculty feeling unprotected, vulnerable, and betrayed. The steadfast avoidance of conflict on the part of this principal allowed a pervasive climate of distrust to emerge. The costs to the school of a culture of distrust included constricted communication, limited access to faculty insights through shared decision making, and reduced organizational citizenship and commitment.

Chapter Five examines revenge and the range of victim responses to betrayal. In this chapter the story is told of Gloria Davies, who took over the reins of an underperforming school determined to make positive change. Her methods, however, were seen as manipulative and unfair; they broke trust with the faculty. These tactics left teachers feeling alienated and distrustful, leading to resentment, power struggles, and sabotage. Her leadership resulted in a school impaired by a culture of control. It is hard to imagine that she will ultimately be successful in achieving the high hopes she had for the school.

In Chapter Six, the leader's role in fostering high-quality relationships among teachers in a school is explored. This chapter also examines some of the positive outcomes of a trusting school environment, such as greater collaboration and a robust sense of collective efficacy that can fuel stronger motivation and persistence.

Chapter Seven examines the dynamics of building trust with students and parents. Barriers to trust can be met and overcome even in a challenging and diverse urban environment. Trust hits schools in their bottom line—student achievement. This chapter reports research that demonstrates this link.

Chapter Eight focuses on the hard work of trust repair and gives practical advice for repairing damaged trust in schools. As school leaders contemplate the high cost of broken trust and the arduous process of rebuilding trust that has been damaged, it may enhance their commitment to build and maintain trust in the first place. Trust is rebuilt through the "four A's of absolution," that is: admit it, apologize, ask forgiveness, and amend your ways. Trust restoration is also facilitated by constructive attitudes, clear boundaries, communication of promises and credible threats, and strategies for conflict resolution.

The final chapter focuses on the behavior of school leaders in becoming trustworthy leaders. Trust plays an important role in principals' functions of visioning, modeling, coaching, managing, and mediating. The advice in this chapter is geared toward helping school leaders harness the powerful resource of trust to make their schools more productive.

In addition to the nine chapters, this book contains several useful appendices. The first includes four trust measures for school leaders and scholars interested in assessing the level of trust in schools. These surveys are accompanied by scoring directions and norms so that practitioners can compare the levels of trust in their schools with typical schools. Another appendix offers suggestions of how principals might address reporting the results to their faculty in a constructive manner. The third appendix provides details about the participants in the study that forms the basis of this book. Finally, an appendix on directions for future research will guide scholars interested in contributing to a greater understanding of the dynamics of this important construct in schools.

There is no simple recipe for fostering trust. Building trust is a complex process requiring reflection and attention to context. The section titled Putting It into Action at the end of each chapter provides practical advice for putting these ideas to work in your school. The key points of each chapter are summarized in a bulleted list for easy reference. The chapter sections titled Questions for Reflection and Discussion invite the reader to explore how these ideas might be applied to trust development in his or her own setting, and might prove helpful to those who want to use this book as a part of a class, professional development series, or collaborative study group.

This book taps into insights from both theory and research across a variety of fields to argue that school leaders need to attend to establishing and maintaining trusting relationships within their schools. It provides practical advice on how to repair damaged trust and helps school leaders learn how they can overcome low trust within their schools and communities to establish effective working relationships. My hope is that this work will serve to ignite greater interest in learning more about the dimensions and dynamics of trustworthy leadership so that school leaders have ever more powerful tools to cultivate trust in schools.

June 2004   MEGAN TSCHANNEN-MORAN

Acknowledgments

I have been blessed to have been surrounded by wonderful and trustworthy people throughout my work on this book—people who are benevolent, honest, open, reliable, and competent. First among these is my husband Bob. Words cannot adequately express my love and appreciation. He is my oldest and dearest friend, as well as a wise and helpful coach. He has sustained me with encouraging words, insightful ideas, mugs of tea, technical assistance, and a ready hug when the going got tough. He took a personal interest not only in helping to edit this book but in applying its concepts. It is exciting to see him using this material in his work with educators through LifeTrek Coaching International.

I have also benefited from a team of friends and colleagues who have read and edited drafts of the chapters and pushed me to make this a better book. These include Jennifer Wallace, Janine Lehane, and Philip Basso. The feedback they offered was always constructive, specific, and helpful. I also want to acknowledge the anonymous reviewers whose helpful insights pushed me to make this book more practical and useful.

I owe a special thanks to all of the contributors who shared their stories of life in school with me. And I want to thank my students at the College of William and Mary who have engaged in dialogue with me around the ideas and issues in this book and helped clarify my thinking with their questions and comments.

In many ways, this book began twenty-five years ago in my journey as the founder and leader of an alternative elementary school in a low-income neighborhood of Chicago. I am indebted to those who joined me on that journey. Taken by the vision of a more wholesome, humane, and effective educational environment for the children of our neighborhood, we created a refreshing oasis in an all too dangerous and dirty corner of the city. For fourteen years, the culture of trust at the school sustained us, often in the face of great adversity. Trust was crucial to the success we had in accomplishing our mission to "unleash the power of education early in the lives of disadvantaged students in order to break the cycle of poverty." The desire to share the lessons learned in that context was impetus for writing this book.

I would not have been as fully able to articulate what made our school so successful had it not been for the guidance of some important teachers along the way. My interest in trust as a topic of study was piqued by the work of my advisor and dissertation chair, Wayne K. Hoy, and led to the study that forms that basis of this book. Wayne has been both a mentor and a friend, and I am grateful for the ways he helped cultivate my interest in research. Anita Woolfolk Hoy has not only been a mentor but also an inspiring role model in both scholarship and teaching. Cynthia Uline is a good friend and wise advisor, and I am blessed by the trust we share. She has been unflagging in her interest in and support of my work on this book. My colleagues at the College of William and Mary are wonderful examples of trustworthy leadership, and I am pleased to work in an environment that reaps the benefits of trust.

I want to thank all of the people at Jossey-Bass who believed in this book enough to see it published. Their gentle pressure coaxed me into making this book more readable, more practical, and more engaging.

Finally, my acknowledgment would not be complete without a special thanks to the people who are dear to me and who have supported me in my work on this book. In addition to my husband, my children Bryn and Evan have been faithful cheerleaders and encouragers throughout the years this book has been in progress. I am also grateful for the steadfast caring and ready ear of my sister, Maura Moran. And it is hard to know what path my life would have taken without the love and generosity of Bob and June Tschannen, but it would not have been as good.

My wish is that everyone would be as richly blessed by trustworthy companions on life's journey as I have been.

Why Trust Matters

I don't ask for much, I only want trust,
And you know, it don't come easy.

Ringo Starr

Sometimes even principals with the best of intentions don't get it right. They are not able to lead their schools into the kind of productive working communities that they imagine and hope for. When these well-intentioned principals fail to earn the trust of their faculty and their larger school communities, their visions are doomed to frustration and failure. Consider the stories of Gloria and Fred, two principals leading schools in the same urban district.

Meaning Well

When Gloria Davies learned that she had been assigned to Lincoln Elementary School, one of the lowest-performing elementary schools in her district, she was determined to turn that school around. She believed that the primarily low-income students at Lincoln, many of whom lived in a nearby housing project, deserved a better education than they were getting. She wanted to implement a new, more powerful and rigorous curriculum, especially in reading. She wanted to get teachers fired up to make the changes that were required to turn the school around. And she was determined to get rid of any teachers that didn't get on board. She believed she owed it to the students. Gloria was fond of saying, "I don't work for the teachers, I work for the students and their families."

Although Gloria is midway through her third year at the school, the school has failed to make the gains that she had hoped for. Gloria is mired in an intense power struggle with the faculty at Lincoln. She has been frustrated by union rules and procedures that have limited her authority. Faculty members have filed numerous union grievances against her for what are perceived as manipulative and heavy-handed methods. Building council meetings, a mechanism for shared decision making mandated by the district, have been reduced to a war of the rule books, each side quoting chapter and verse from the district contract or the union guidelines to bolster their position. Although Gloria has been successful in removing one untenured teacher, her attempts to remove veteran teachers have been met with resistance and rebellion that have gone well beyond the targeted teachers. Morale is extremely low, and student achievement scores have not risen significantly. In a self-protective move, Gloria confines herself to her office and is rarely seen about the school except to make unscheduled observations of teachers she is trying to remove. Unfortunately, Gloria's dreams of turning around this failing school have not materialized, because her methods have cost her the trust of her faculty and have led to resentment, power struggles, and sabotage.

Fred Martin, principal of Fremont Elementary, a few miles from Lincoln, is a friendly man with a warm smile and an easy-going disposition. He is generally well-liked by the teachers, students, and parents in his community. He is sympathetic to the difficult circumstances that many of his low-income students face, as well as the stresses inherent in teaching in an urban context. Fred considers himself a progressive principal, and delegates many important and controversial decisions to the building council. He views his low-key role with the council as empowering teachers as decision makers in the school. He sees himself as fair-minded and can usually see both sides of a conflict. Consequently, he is reluctant to make a decision that will be perceived as favoring one side or the other. He is disappointed that his students have done so poorly on the state assessments but feels that policymakers should be made to understand the challenges that he and his teachers face.

Fred's discomfort with and avoidance of conflict has not made for an absence of conflict at Fremont. On the contrary, without direct efforts to address conflict productively, discord and disagreements have escalated. Teachers feel angry and unsupported by Fred when they send misbehaving students to him for discipline and perceive that they receive little more than a fatherly chat. Teachers in conflict with one another are left to their own devices to resolve their differences. When they go to Fred, he wants to avoid taking sides and so avoids making any kind of judgment at all. Instead he refers them to the building council or tells them simply that they are going to need to work things out. As a result, long-standing grudges between teachers have simmered for years. Bitterness between the teachers and the teacher aides, many of whom are parents hired from the neighborhood, has become an entrenched part of the school culture. Teachers perceive that the aides are lazy and are not made to do the job they were hired to do, whereas the aides find the teachers unwelcoming, demanding, and rude. In the meantime, student achievement has failed to significantly improve, despite the increasing pressure of state and district accountability measures.

Though well intentioned, neither Gloria nor Fred has been successful at shaping a constructive school environment. What is missing in both circumstances is trust. Because neither principal is regarded as trustworthy by his or her faculty, neither has positive results to show for her and his efforts. On the one hand, Gloria, the overzealous reformer, was too impatient for change to foster the kinds of relationships she would need to align her faculty with the lofty vision she had for the school. Her heavy-handed tactics were seen as betrayals by the teachers in her school. Fred, on the other hand, in trying to keep the peace by avoiding conflict, lost the trust of his faculty through benign neglect. His attempts to keep everybody happy resulted in a general malaise and perpetual undercurrent of unresolved tension in the school. Although teachers liked Fred and felt they could count on his sympathetic concern, they could not count on him to take action on their behalf because of his fear of making someone else angry. His teachers were left feeling vulnerable and unprotected.

These two principals are real-life examples of how principals often respond to resistance to change among their faculty by either overasserting their authority or withdrawing from the fray (Sarason, 1982). Both responses damage trust, and both hamper a principal's ability to lead. Gloria focused too narrowly on the task of school improvement and neglected the relationships that she needed to cultivate to get the job done. Although she is correct in thinking that her primary responsibility is for the education of her students, not for the comfort and ease of her teachers, she has failed to grasp that principals necessarily get their jobs done through other people. Fred, in contrast, has focused too much on relationships at the expense of the task. But because the task involves protecting the well-being of the members of the school community, Fred's avoidance of conflict has damaged the relationships he sought to enhance. By withdrawing, Fred has failed to provide the leadership, structure, and training to provide a quality education for the students in his care.

Both Fred and Gloria can also be seen as demonstrating problems of responsibility (Martin, 2002). Gloria has taken on too much responsibility for the change initiative in her school and so has interfered with teachers getting on board and taking ownership in the process. In vigorously asserting her authority, Gloria has made her point all too well that teachers are not in charge and do not have a say in the decisions that vitally affect their work life. Her actions have violated the sense of care that teachers expect from their principal and caused them to question her integrity. Their trust in her has been damaged. Fred has taken too little responsibility, handing decisions over to teachers they do not have the expertise to make. He has not supported them adequately through mentoring and training to acquire the skills to contribute to the decisions necessary to run the school. He has not demonstrated the competence and reliability necessary to build trust, and so is not seen as trustworthy by his faculty and school community.

The problems these two principals evidence are not unusual. New principals, like Gloria, often feel the need to enter a school setting and create change. Inexperienced principals tend to be unsure of their authority and, as a result, a common mistake among novice school leaders is to be fairly forceful in establishing their authority within the school. Barth (1981) observed that, "Most people I know who are beginning principals enter their new roles as advocates, friends, helpers, supporters, often former colleagues of teachers. By December of their first year they have become adversaries, requirers, forcers, judges, and setters of limits" (p. 148). This approach can be counterproductive when trying to develop a high-trust school. Building trust requires patience and planning, whereas novice principals tend to have a "do it now" attitude.

Fred, however, apparently lacked important leadership skills such as conflict resolution skills and professional development training. Perhaps he also lacked the courage and the stamina to face the sometimes uncomfortable aspects of school leadership and especially school change. When he ran into resistance, he withdrew. Although empowering teachers to participate in important decisions within the school can be an effective means to reach higher-quality decisions, Fred needed to provide the leadership and training to help his teachers be successful at shared leadership. The teachers and students in his school needed more than a sympathetic ear to help resolve the conflicts they faced. They needed someone who could structure a process that would lead to productive solutions.

Doing Well

Although these two scenarios are not uncommon, principals need
not follow either path. Brenda Thompson is principal of Brookside
Elementary, a school that serves a student body similar to those at
Lincoln and Fremont in the same urban district. Through trustworthy leadership, Brenda has earned the confidence of her faculty.
By balancing a strong sense of care for the students and teachers of
her school with high performance expectations, Brenda has fostered
a schoolwide culture of trust. Responsibility for school improvement
is shared. By working hard herself, Brenda sets an example and is
able to command an extra measure of effort from her teachers.
These efforts have been rewarded with above-average performance
from Brookside students on measures of student achievement.

Brenda's care for her faculty and students is evidenced in her
accessibility. Brenda is rarely in her office during the school day, pre-
ferring to spend her time in the hallways, classrooms, and cafeteria.
She spends lunch recess on the playground. She is available to assist
teachers and students as they engage in problem solving around the
difficulties they face. She is a trusted advisor who listens well. She
offers thoughtful and useful suggestions that demonstrate her expertise as an educator. She doesn't blame or make the teacher feel
incompetent for having a problem or not knowing what to do. Her
caring extends beyond the walls of the school; teachers, students,
and parents seek her out for help with their lives outside of school as
well. The tone of caring set by Brenda is echoed in the faculty's care
for one another and for their students. The impetus for school improvement stems from this caring atmosphere. Caring fuels the
enormous effort needed to sustain a positive school environment in
this challenging context.

Brenda understands that the work of schools happens primarily
through relationships, so she invests time and resources in nurturing those relationships. There are a number of annual traditions
that foster good rapport, not just among the faculty but among the

students and their families as well. Brenda makes use of a local high-ropes course twice a year for a challenging, team-building experience with the third through fifth graders and their teachers. Parents are also invited along for the fun. Brenda wears jeans and hiking boots and joins right in, an amusing contrast for the students to her normally professional dress. An important community-building tradition at the school is an annual fall sleepover called Camp Night, when students and their parents, in mixed grade-level groups, participate in fun, hands-on learning experiences, have a meal provided by the Parent Teacher Association (PTA), and sleep at the school. Brenda structures time for the faculty to work together and share ideas and resources, allowing grade-level teams common planning time most days. The school is not free of conflict, but the strong sense of community supports the constructive resolution of the inevitable differences.

We can learn much about the vital role of trustworthy school leadership from the stories of these three principals. They are real principals, although their names have been changed and the distinguishing characteristics of their schools disguised. The voices of the teachers in their schools throughout the book are taken from actual interviews. The sidebar vignettes come from encounters with teachers and parents as well as exchanges with my students over the years I have been teaching and writing on this topic.

Principals and other school leaders need to earn the trust of the stakeholders in their school communities if they are to be successful. They need to understand how trust is built and how it is lost. Getting smarter about trust will help school leaders foster more successful schools.

Trust and Schools

When we turn a nostalgic eye toward schools in an earlier era, it seems that there was once a time that schools enjoyed the implicit trust of their communities. School leaders were highly respected and largely unquestioned members of the community. Teachers were regarded as having valuable professional knowledge about how children learn and what was best for them. When a child was punished at school, parents accepted and reinforced the judgment of school officials. If those days ever really did exist, they are not what many who work in schools are currently experiencing.

It is important that school leaders not take the general distrust of their schools too personally. It is part of a larger pattern in society, shaped by economic, political, and social forces. We now live in an era when all of our social institutions are under unprecedented scrutiny. We are barraged by a steady stream of media attention to scandals, revealing how business leaders, politicians, church leaders, nonprofit executives, and school leaders have acted from self-interest rather than out of the interests of the constituents whom they purport to serve. These revelations erode the trust we once held for these institutions and undermine their basic legitimacy.

We tend to notice trust most when it has been damaged or destroyed (Baier, 1994). These days, it seems evident that trust in our society has indeed been injured. As life has grown more complex, as changing economic realities and changing expectations in society have made life less predictable, and as new forms of information dissemination have increased both the availability and desire for negative information, we are beginning to *notice* trust much more. In the midst of the media blitz of bad news, trust has emerged as a favorite theme of advertisers in promoting everything from investment firms to hair salons. Many seem to be longing for the days when trust came more easily.

Changing Expectations

Changed economic realities and social problems have led to mounting pressures on schools. Economically, the shift toward a more global economy has increased competition and forced changes in the outcomes society expects of schools. This economic shift has diminished the proportion of low-skilled jobs in developed countries. Our economy is dependent on a more highly skilled workforce and on a larger proportion of students who earn a high school diploma. Graduates must be proficient not just in basic skills but also in the ability to reason and solve complex problems. They must be able to work well in groups or teams, as the problems they will be likely to experience in the workplace will be too complex to be solved by an individual working alone. Schools are expected to provide a stronger workforce for continued economic competitiveness in a global marketplace. Although much of the criticism of schools in the popular media has been overblown, and our schools are doing a much better job than is frequently reported, pressure is being brought to bear on schools to adapt to a changing world (Berliner & Biddle, 1995).

Equity

Social changes evident now include a greater awareness of inequality on the part of the average person. As more people have access to more information, they also gain greater consciousness of the discrepancies in opportunities and outcomes available to people from differing social strata. In our society, the value of equality has taken on ever-greater importance. Students take seriously the expectation of equal opportunities and the right of all citizens to participate in economic prosperity.

There is an increasing desire of the less powerful to have more control over those whose greater power vitally affects them. The ever more powerful knowledge possessed by professionals influences both individual and public welfare (Barber, 1983). With greater access to information through the Internet, many people are no longer content to accept the role of passive client. Doctors are finding that many of their patients are engaging in independent research about their conditions and come with detailed questions and recommendations for their treatment. Lawyers are encountering more clients who have read up on legal precedents and maneuvers that might be helpful to their case. Parents, too, are conducting

research and feeling ever more empowered as their children's advocates within the system and to question the professional knowledge
and expertise of school personnel.

With increasing expectations and the disappointment of many
of those expectations, trust in our schools has been damaged (Kozol,
1991; Tyack & Cuban, 1995). In some ways, these dashed hopes
and distrust are the result of the very success of public schools, with
the increased knowledge and reasoning skills that a better educated
public brings to its relations with professionals, experts, and other
leaders. The success of our educational system has created the very
conditions that enable the common person to think critically and
to challenge the status quo. Consequently, better education has
created greater need for trustworthiness on the part of leaders and
professionals.

Much of the responsibility for realizing our society's vision of
greater equity is vested in our schools. Consequently, higher expectations are especially brought to bear on those who educate our children. The actions of school professionals influence not just our
children's current welfare but also their future educational and economic potential. Previously, schools functioned largely to sort and
rank students for various strata of society. Notable exceptions helped
to maintain the belief in our society as a meritocracy, where anyone
with the ability and work ethic could overcome the deficiencies of
their origins and prosper economically or politically. However,
schools largely maintained the status quo in terms of social rank and
prosperity. That role has come under attack and has largely been
supplanted by the goal of fostering greater equality of opportunity
and outcomes for all students, even those with disabilities and those
from lower socioeconomic strata (Goodlad, 1984).

Schools, however, struggle to realize these new aspirations, especially those schools that serve high-poverty populations. A half-
century after the *Brown* v. *Board of Education* decision to desegregate
public schools, the dream of schools eliminating race and class distinctions and of providing equal opportunities to learn seems far

from becoming reality. As educators are charged with reducing the effects of economic disparities in our society, schools are increasingly feeling the brunt of public distrust. The professional knowledge possessed by educators is held suspect as much touted innovations (for example, open classrooms or new math) failed to bring the dramatic results they promised (Tyack & Cuban, 1995). In addition, the values promoted by schools may be at odds with the conflicted values of a diverse society (Macedo, 2000).

Pressure for Change

In this time of societal and economic flux, political forces are brought to bear to pressure schools into making the necessary changes to meet our new, loftier goals for them. There is an urgency to identify and repair the problems that plague low-performing schools. As Gloria has learned, however, urgency is not enough to turn around a failing school. Standards have been imposed on schools because educators were not consistently accountable, thereby forfeiting the public's trust. Negative publicity has been used to shift schools from complacency to compliance with new accountability measures. Principals like Fred, however, resist and resent these measures when they don't have the means and know-how to foster a productive school culture. Principals like Gloria become impatient with the slow pace of change and try to force rapid change upon their reluctant faculty, generating resistance and resentment instead of improved outcomes. It takes the wisdom of a principal like Brenda to patiently apply both support and challenge to lead a school toward fruitful change.

Putting It into Action

Schools must garner trust and legitimacy in an era when these commodities are in short supply within the society at large. To be a trustworthy school leader, you must learn to create the conditions for trust to flourish within your school as well as between your school and your community. School leaders who, like Brenda, earn the trust of the members of their school community are in a better position to accomplish the complex task of educating a diverse group of students in a changing world. Principals and teachers who trust each other can better work together in the service of solving the challenging problems of schooling. These leaders create a bond that helps inspire teachers to move to higher levels of effort and achievement. These leaders also create the conditions that foster trust between teachers, including structures and norms for behavior, and they assist them in resolving the inevitable conflicts that arise.

As citizens have become increasingly distrustful of their institutions and leaders, the trend away from trust creates a special challenge for schools because trust is so fundamental to their core mission. Schools need the trust of the parents who send their children to school, as well as that of the communities that sponsor and fund them. In order to learn, students must trust their teachers because, for much of what is learned in schools, students are asked to believe what teachers tell them and what they read without independent evidence. Students who do not trust their teachers or each other will be likely to divert energy into self-protection and away from engagement with the learning task. Moreover, students who do not feel trusted by their teachers and administrators may create barriers to learning as they distance themselves from schools and build an alienated, rebellious youth culture. They may, in fact, live down to the low expectations of a distrustful school environment. As a trustworthy school leader, you must model trusting relationships with students and parents and serve as an example for teachers to cultivate these trusting relationships as well.

Trust can no longer be taken for granted in schools. It must be conscientiously cultivated and sustained. As a school leader, you bear the largest responsibility for setting a tone of trust in your schools. It is time for school leaders to become knowledgeable about cultivating trust because trustworthy leadership is at the heart of successful schools.

Key Points About Why Trust Matters

- School leaders that have the trust of their communities are more likely to be successful in creating productive learning environments.

- Trust is a challenge for schools at this point in history, when all of our institutions are under unprecedented scrutiny.

- Much of the responsibility for realizing our society's vision of greater equity is vested in our schools. Consequently, higher expectations are especially brought to bear on those who educate our children.

- Without trust, schools are likely to flounder in their attempts to provide constructive educational environments and meet the lofty goals that our society has set for them because energy needed to solve the complex problem of educating a diverse group of students is diverted into self-protection.

- Trustworthy leadership is the heart of productive schools.

Questions for Reflection and Discussion

1. What are the signs that trust is either present or absent in your school? What are the effects you notice of the presence or absence of trust?

2. How do you know whether you are taking the appropriate amount of responsibility for continuous school improvement in your school? What skills and support do you need to provide teachers so they can assume a meaningful role in the change process? How can you avoid becoming discouraged by the inevitable resistance to change?

3. What steps can you take to foster trusting relationships between your school and your community when there is so much bad publicity about schools in the media?

2

What Is Trust?

Trust is the assurance that one can count on the good
will of another to act in one's best interest.

Baier (1994)

Trust matters because single-handedly we can neither create nor
sustain many of the things we care most about. Trust is mani-
fest in situations in which we must rely on the competence of others and their willingness to look after what is precious to us. Because
we must allow others to help us care for what we cherish, they are
placed in positions in which they can, if they choose, injure what
we value (Baier, 1994). As a society we invest much of what we
cherish most in our schools. We send our children to schools, trusting that they will be safe from harm, as well as guided and taught in
keeping with our highest hopes for them. Schools are also invested
with a significant share of our collective resources in the form of tax
dollars, school buildings, and local employment opportunities. In
addition, schools are charged with keeping and promoting our
shared values and ideals. They foster and protect our ideals of respect, tolerance, and democracy, as well as the vision of equity in
our society (Macedo, 2000). It is evident why trust has become a
pressing issue for schools.

Trust has paradoxically been viewed as both a glue and a lubricant. As "glue" trust binds organizational participants to one

another. Without it, things fall apart. To be productive and to accomplish organizational goals, schools need cohesive and cooperative relationships. Trust is essential to fostering these relationships (Baier, 1994; Goldring & Rallis, 1993; Louis, Kruse, & Marks, 1996). Trust binds leaders to followers. Without that bond, a manager can enforce minimum compliance with contract specifications and job descriptions, but that will not lead a team of teachers into greatness. As "lubricant," trust greases the machinery of an organization. Trust "lubricates" communication and contributes to greater efficiency when people can have confidence in other people's words and deeds (Arrow, 1974). Without trust, friction and "heat" are generated that bog down the work of the school. Energy is expended in making provisions against possible or feared betrayal by the other party. Schools need trust to foster communication and facilitate efficiency.

Trust is also a choice. Trust is a judgment based on evidence, but it outstrips the evidence that would rationally justify it. The trusting party makes this leap of faith out of care for the relationship. Solomon and Flores (2001) note that trust is "cultivated through speech, conversation, commitments, and action. Trust is never something 'already at hand,' it is always a matter of human effort. It can and often must be conscientiously created, not simply taken for granted" (p. 87). These authors assert that it is unethical to withhold trust without good reason just as it is unethical to treat a person unfairly in other ways.

Trust within schools can be fostered or diminished by the behavior of the leader. Schools that cultivate trust can reap the benefits of greater adaptability and innovation as well as reduced costs (Mishra, 1996). Unfortunately, the very conditions conducive to the emergence of trust also allow for its abuse (Elangovan & Shapiro, 1998). Despite the dividends of a culture of trust, organizational dynamics often complicate things because the power differences imposed by hierarchical relationships add complexity to interpersonal interactions. School leaders can overcome these potential barriers through genuine caring and steadfast commitment combined with thoughtful action and initiative.

Defining Trust

Most people rely on an intuitive feel of what is meant when we say that we *trust* someone. Trust is difficult to define because it is so complex. It is a multifaceted construct, meaning that there are many elements or drivers of an overall level of trust. Trust may vary somewhat depending on the context of the trust relationship. It is also dynamic in that it can change over the course of a relationship, as expectations are either fulfilled or disappointed and as the nature of the interdependence between two people changes. Reoccurring themes emerged as I examined various definitions of trust in the literature, which led me to the following definition: *Trust is one's willingness to be vulnerable to another based on the confidence that the other is benevolent, honest, open, reliable, and competent* (Mishra, 1996; Tschannen-Moran & Hoy, 1998, 2000).

Vulnerability

Trust matters most in situations of interdependence, in which the interests of one party cannot be achieved without reliance upon another. Unless parties are dependent on one another for something they care about or need, trust is not critical. But interdependence brings with it vulnerability. Trust is the extent to which one is willing to rely upon and make oneself vulnerable to another (Baier, 1994; Bigley & Pearce, 1998). The one who trusts recognizes the potential for betrayal and harm from the other. Trust is not an issue in situations where one has complete control over the actions of another. The uncertainty concerning whether the other intends to and will act appropriately entails taking a risk (Rousseau, Sitkin, Burt, & Camerer, 1998; Solomon & Flores, 2001). Taking the risk requires trust, which in turn buttresses the development of trust when the expected behavior materializes.

One of the early puzzles that emerged in the study of trust was whether it was an individual's behavior or attitude in a situation of vulnerability that mattered. For example, when a parent leaves her young child at school but holds significant misgivings about doing so, can the parent be said to have trusted the school? By taking action, the parent has voluntarily increased her risk for negative outcomes; however, she has done so with a certain level of anxiety. The decision to place oneself at risk to another could be based on many motivations, including need, hope, conformity, innocence, impulsivity, masochism, or confidence (Deutsch, 1960). Although the behavior of the parent who anxiously left her child at school was the same as that of a parent with no such misgivings, the level of trust is very different. There is growing consensus that trust lies in the degree of confidence one holds in the face of risk rather than in the choice or action that increases one's risk (Rousseau et al., 1998). Trust, then, is the "accepted vulnerability to another's possible but not expected ill will" (Baier, 1994, p. 99).

Schools ask for the trust of parents, not just to protect the children in their care but also to shape their thinking and behavior. Students are expected to leave school altered, presumably better, than when they entered. Schools also ask for their community to risk vulnerability by sharing a major portion of the community's collective resources in the form of tax dollars and school buildings, as well as for control of significant employment opportunities within the community. Schools and school personnel require great trust because of what is at stake if schools perform poorly. Poor school performance has serious negative consequences both for the individual students and for the community as a whole.

Facets of Trust

Teachers and principals are interdependent in their shared project of educating the students in their school. As such they are vulnerable to one another. Therefore, the principal-teacher relationship provides a window into the trust dynamics within a school. In

Brenda we have an excellent example of a trustworthy school leader. Her story and those of Gloria and Fred illustrate the various facets that people rely upon in making trust judgments. Each of the facets of trust—benevolence, honesty, openness, reliability, and competence—is played out in the relationships within these schools.

Benevolence

Perhaps the most essential ingredient and commonly recognized facet of trust is a sense of caring or benevolence; the confidence that one's well-being or something one cares about will be protected and not harmed by the trusted party (Baier, 1994; Zand, 1997). Trust rests on the assurance that one can count on the good will of another to act in one's best interest, that the other will not exploit one's vulnerability even when the opportunity is available (Cummings & Bromily, 1996). In a situation in which one is dependent upon and consequently vulnerable to another, faith in the caring intentions or altruism of the other is particularly important. Parents who trust educators to care for their children are confident that the educators will consistently act with the best interests of their children in mind; that their children will be treated not only with fairness but with compassion. In an ongoing relationship, the future actions or deeds required for continued trust may not be specified, only that there will be a mutual attitude of good will (Putnam, 2000). There is a sense of care, not just care about the immediate outcome but also care about the relationship. People make emotional investments in trust relationships and believe that these sentiments are reciprocated (McAllister, 1995).

When trust in the benevolence of others is missing, there is likely to be a cost in overall productivity as energy is invested in making mental provisions or alternative plans or in assessing the available recourse in case of betrayal. Students who do not trust their teachers or fellow students cannot learn efficiently because they invest their energy in calculating ways to protect themselves instead of engaging in the learning process. If stories about how an administrator has failed to reliably protect the interests of a teacher or student circulate, a cycle of mistrust may begin to form as people begin to fear that they, too, might be victimized.

School leaders can promote trust by demonstrating benevolence: showing consideration and sensitivity for employees' needs and interests, acting in a way that protects employees' rights, and refraining from exploiting others for personal gain. Brenda demonstrated benevolence in a variety of ways at Brookside. David, a midcareer teacher who had taught at Brookside for nine years, described the importance of Brenda's good will or benevolence and its impact on teachers: "I think her underlying motivation is to help you be the best that you can be at what you are doing. Her underlying desire for you is nothing but good. She is always looking for ways to build you up, to let you know what your strengths are. And then areas she sees maybe you need to work on—giving you ways to work on those or see how others do it. She expects a lot but she gives a lot." Teachers were more willing to give the extra measure and meet the high demands that Brenda placed on them because of the level of support they received.

One of the ways that Brenda demonstrated support for her faculty was in consistently expressing appreciation for their hard work. Simple expressions of appreciation went a long way toward building satisfaction and commitment among the faculty in Brenda's building. Christy, another teacher at Brookside described what even small expressions of gratitude meant to her. "Brenda's expectations are very, very high. We spend a lot of hours after school, on weekends; we work a lot more than some other schools. However, she is always very appreciative. The next day there is always a comment in the bulletin saying, "Thank you those of you who attended the program last night." We are in a very thankless job. Parents don't often say thank you, and kids don't come up and say, 'Thank you for teaching me!' But at least she does it. And that's all I need. I just need a little bit of acknowledgment."

Because of the support these teachers received from Brenda, they were willing to accept correction from her and to work hard to meet the high expectations she had for them. Kathy, a teacher in her fifth year at Brookside, voiced these sentiments. "Even though sometimes she gets mad and yells at us, we take our lickings and we go on. Yet, when we have a problem and we ask her for assistance she is right there to give it to us."

Reputations serve either to strengthen high trust or diminish low trust. Social networks tend to drive trust relationships toward extremes, enhancing strong trust relationships and compounding the effects of broken trust (Burt & Knez, 1996). Where trust is high, newer members in the social system are encouraged to extend trust even when events might otherwise have caused them to be guarded. At Brookside, although Brenda could occasionally be short-tempered or "snippy," new faculty members were coached by their peers not to let an occasional display of temper or a negative remark on Brenda's part interfere with developing a sense of trust. They were told that because she cared so much and worked so hard for the school, it was understandable that she would sometimes be tired and irritable. Newcomers were assured that if they ever needed help or support of any kind they could count on Brenda. This willingness to forgive Brenda her shortcomings was enhanced by the story that Brenda, when confronted with a teacher with hurt feelings, had been willing to apologize for a short-tempered remark. The story enhanced trust even among those teachers who had never been the recipient of such an apology.

In situations of high trust, people do not hesitate to seek help because they do not fear that others will think they are inadequate. They will not feel threatened by being seen as dependent upon another person or be as concerned about incurring indebtedness to another person (Jones & George, 1998). High-trust principals often extend their care beyond the scope of school, with a willingness to listen and advise teachers about issues they faced in the personal realm. Principals who hope to earn the trust of their faculties need to demonstrate good will and genuine concern for teachers' well-being.

One important distinction: trust is not the same as liking a person. It is possible to like someone you do not trust and trust someone you do not especially like. Because caring is an element of trust and we tend to like those from whom we feel benevolence or goodwill, it may be more likely that you will trust those you like and like those you trust. But affection is not necessary for trust to develop.

Honesty

Honesty is a fundamental facet of trust (Butler & Cantrell, 1984; Cummings & Bromily, 1996). Honesty concerns a person's character, their integrity, and authenticity. Trust means that one can expect that the word or promise of another individual, whether verbal or written, can be relied upon (Rotter, 1967). Trust implies that statements made were truthful and conformed to "what really happened," at least from that person's perspective, and that commitments made about future actions will be kept. Without the confidence that a person's words can be relied upon and can accurately predict future actions, trust is unlikely to develop.

People earn a reputation of integrity from telling the truth and keeping promises (Dasgupta, 1988). Correspondence between a person's statements and deeds characterizes integrity. Integrity is the perceived match between a person's values as expressed in words and those expressed through action—in other words, between their talk and their walk (Simons,

OUR PRINCIPAL'S EYES popped out when he saw the teachers' year-end evaluation of our new assistant principal. "Wow!" he said, "What has she done with the teachers?" But you know what? You can always go in her office and talk to her. You can bring her an issue you are dealing with and she goes right into a problem-solving mode. It never, ever comes back to bite you—like you are incompetent or can't do your job. The teachers really appreciate that.

John, second grade teacher

1999). When a person says one thing yet does another, trust is compromised. Trust might survive a broken promise if an explanation is given; however, a pattern of broken promises will be likely to provoke a serious threat to trust.

When school leaders unveil a new vision or change initiative for the school but then do not follow through, change course again, or do not uphold the principles of their own program, it is worse than if they had not begun in the first place. The "flavor of the month" syndrome creates cynicism and damages trust rather than leading to positive, sustainable change. When Gloria first arrived at Lincoln, the speeches she gave to the faculty seemed to promise a new day for the school, but as she became mired in conflict at the school those implicit and explicit promises crumbled.

In an effort to please everyone or avoid conflict, administrators sometimes fail to be completely honest and upfront with individuals. Fred frequently made statements that he was not going to tolerate certain behaviors, such as the continual tardiness of certain faculty members or the abuse of sick days. But when his actions failed to correspond to his tough words and nothing was done to address the inappropriate behaviors, the faculty lost faith in Fred's integrity. Failure to follow through on a threat or consequence can be as damaging to trust as a broken promise. The object of the threat may be pleased or relieved not to have the threat fulfilled, but the disconnect between the person's actions and words damages trust.

The revelation of dishonest behavior may be more damaging to trust than lapses in other facets because it is read as an indictment of the person's character. Once a principal has been caught in even a single lie and the faculty has lost faith in the word of their principal, trust can be difficult to reestablish because the communication tool necessary to restore trust is now suspect. Simons (1999) warns: "Words are one of a manager's most potent tools for guiding subordinates. . . . When credibility is sacrificed, the manager damages that tool, and is forced into additional actions to show when he or she 'really means' what he or she says" (p. 95).

Authentic behavior consists of three basic aspects: accountability, avoiding manipulation, and being "real" rather than seeming to play a preconceived role (Henderson & Hoy, 1982; Tschannen-Moran & Hoy, 1998). Accountability is characterized by an acceptance of responsibility for one's actions and avoidance of distorting the truth in order to shift blame to another. There is no passing the buck, scapegoating, or finger pointing at others. This means the willingness to accept responsibility not just for good things that happen, but for mistakes and negative outcomes as well. Rather than protecting his or her reputation as hoped, a principal who continually tries to cover his or her own shortcomings and mistakes by shifting blame to others will be more likely to earn the distrust of both teachers and superiors.

Authenticity also reflects the perception of individuals that their leaders avoid exploiting or using them. Authentic leaders treat others as people, to be respected as persons rather than as pawns to be manipulated. In addition, authentic leaders are able to break through the barriers of role stereotyping and behave in ways that are consistent with their true self. Their basic personality is a prime motivator of behavior, not their idea of how to play some prescribed role. Although Gloria had good intentions in relation to turning around Lincoln School, she failed when it came to authenticity. She seemed all too ready to shift blame to her teachers when things did not go smoothly. For example, Gloria's teachers felt hurt and betrayed when they overheard her blaming the teachers for a failed grant proposal, even though she had been a member of the committee that had written the proposal and had not carried her

OUR PRINCIPAL RARELY gets into classrooms to observe or give feedback. But when we had our accreditation visit, right in front of the whole team our principal said that he gets into every classroom at least once a year, if not more. He said that most were informal, drop-in visits. We all knew that it wasn't true. We couldn't believe he would come right out and lie like that! After that, I never trusted him in the same way again.

Kim, high school science teacher

weight in the writing process. Her faculty also saw her as manipulative in her attempts to move people around and to remove teachers who were not immediately compliant or did not bend to her will. As tensions mounted, her self-protective move of withdrawal to the safety of her office left her little chance to interact with teachers in informal, congenial ways that would allow for her basic personality and character to be revealed.

Openness

Openness is a process by which people make themselves vulnerable to others by sharing information, influence, and control (Zand, 1997). Openness in information means disclosure of facts, alternatives, judgments, intentions, and feelings. Openness in control accepts dependence rooted in a confidence in the reliability of others and delegation of important tasks to them. Openness in influence allows others to initiate change to plans, goals, concepts, criteria, and resources. When leaders make themselves vulnerable through these forms of openness, a spiral of trust is initiated that serves to foster increasing levels of trust in the organization. Openness initiates a kind of reciprocal trust, signaling a confidence that neither the information nor the individual will be exploited, so that recipients infer that they can feel the same confidence in return. In taking the initiative to make yourself vulnerable by engaging in acts of trust, the hope is that you may be able to induce others to do the same (Kramer, Brewer, & Hanna, 1996).

Sharing information increases vulnerability because with knowledge comes power. When principals exchange thoughts and ideas freely with teachers, it not only enhances perceptions of trust but leads to greater openness on the part of teachers as well (Butler, 1991). Teachers are more willing to share their thoughts, feelings, and ideas, thus making these valuable resources available for school improvement (Zand, 1997). The information shared is a giving of yourself, whether it is strictly about organizational matters or whether you choose to share personal information (Butler &

Cantrell, 1984; Mishra, 1996). Teachers see principals as trustworthy when their communication is both accurate and forthcoming (Bryk & Schneider, 2002). Adequate explanations and timely feedback on decisions lead to higher trust (Sapienza & Korsgaard, 1996).

Fostering open communication can provide a strategic advantage for schools. In schools with a greater level of trust, teachers and other staff members are more likely to disclose more accurate, relevant, and complete data about problems. Where communication flows freely, problems can be disclosed, diagnosed, and corrected before they are compounded. Teachers function as an early warning system by making the principal aware of problems while they are still small. Because of her accessibility and openness, Brenda was made aware of small problems brewing in the school so that they could be addressed before they escalated. Principals who want to encourage candor among their staff members must cultivate an atmosphere of trust, which means actively encouraging teachers to voice their frustrations candidly, including criticisms of the principal's own decisions.

Openness in communication needs to take place in the context of good judgment. It is a critical element of trustworthy leadership to maintain strict standards of confidentiality. School leaders may not be able to explain or defend their decisions or actions when doing so would require sharing confidential information. One of the more painful experiences some administrative interns encounter in their journey toward becoming school leaders is to have to bite their tongues in the face of criticism from others who do not have all of the relevant information. It is also important at all times to "speak with good purpose" (Reina & Reina, 1999), that is, to refrain from engaging in gossip, small-minded chatter, faultfinding, or other forms of negativity.

Withholding important information is one way that leaders maintain power or manipulate employees (Gabarro, 1978; Kramer, 1996; Mishra, 1996). People who are guarded in the information they share provoke suspicion because people wonder what is being hidden and why. Just as openness breeds trust, suspiciousness breeds distrust. People who are never willing to extend trust through openness can end up living in isolated prisons of their own making (Kramer et al., 1996). A principal who is secretive about her whereabouts and withholds relevant information in order to retain control over who has what information is unlikely to garner the trust of her faculty. For example, the year the interviews were conducted at Brookside, Lincoln, and Fremont, a new superintendent in the district was gathering all the principals to the central office for weekly meetings. Whereas Brenda's faculty at Brookside directed their anger toward the superintendent for this disruption because they missed having her in the building, Gloria did not feel that she owed her faculty an explanation of her whereabouts so the faculty suspected that the meetings were a fabrication and that she was simply shirking her responsibilities.

When administrators share influence and control, they demonstrate significant trust and respect for their teachers (Hoy & Tarter, 2003; Leonard, 1999; Short & Greer, 1997). They must be willing to make themselves vulnerable by sharing authority and the consequences for joint actions that are taken. Delegating authority to teachers and joint deliberation in decision making not only foster trust in schools, they also promote a greater spirit of professional community (Louis, Kruse, & Associates, 1995; Marks & Louis, 1997).

Although not all decision making was relinquished to the

THERE IS A high level of trust in our whole school district. It starts with our superintendent, who has an open door policy. That sets a tone that is mirrored throughout the central office and among all of the principals in the district. There is a feeling that you don't have to be afraid to take risks here—and if it doesn't work out, you won't be blasted. He'll just ask you what you learned from the experience so you don't have to learn that lesson again.

Barbara, curriculum director

faculty at Brookside School, Brenda included faculty members in decision making in a way that maintained a sense of accountability to the mission and goals of the school. Kathy described the process this way:

> She polls our opinions a lot. Sometimes she has made a few decisions on her own that we haven't always agreed with, but for the most are part she'll come to us and say, "What do you think?" If we come to her and say we have this idea, we have to have a solution for how it will work. If you come with an idea and a plan for making it work, then she is very open to it and she will think about it. Our input is very important to what happens— because we have to do it. We have to teach it and we have to implement it.

Brenda's willingness to allow for faculty input was evident in a decision concerning the arrangements of classrooms in the school. The faculty wanted to change the physical layout of the classrooms to allow grade-level teams to work more closely together and share supplies. Brenda, however, wanted to keep a mixture of grade levels near each other to support the program of having older students "buddy up" with younger students. When the faculty came up with a compromise plan that could accommodate both sets of needs by mixing only those grade levels that partnered together on each hall, Brenda implemented the change.

Reliability

It is not enough to show support from time to time or to demonstrate benevolence sporadically. The sense that one is able to depend on another consistently is an important element of trust. Teachers may conclude that their principal is a nice person and means well, and even that he or she is very capable and helpful if you can get his or her attention. But if overcommitment, trouble

managing the time demands of
the job, or a tendency to be easily distracted means teachers
cannot count on the principal to
come through for them when
needed, trust will not characterize the relationship.

Trust has to do with predictability, that is, knowing what to
expect from others; but in and of
itself predictability is inadequate
as a facet of trust. We can expect
a person to be invariably late
or we can count on someone to
be consistently malicious, self-

WE REALLY MISS our old principal. When
you would ask him something, he would
say, "Let me think about it and I'll get
back to you." And he always would. He
was just very thoughtful and deliberative
in his decisions. Our new principal will
make decisions right on the spot. But
then when she gets more information or
somebody complains, she changes it. We
never know what the final decision is or
when it might change. It leaves everybody guessing.

Nicole, fifth grade teacher

serving, or dishonest. When our well-being is diminished or damaged in a predictable way, our expectations may be met but we do
not really trust the other party, although our language may seem to
indicate we do ("You can trust John to blow it!"). Reliability, or
dependability, combines a sense of predictability with caring. In a
situation of interdependence, when something is required from
another person or group, the individual can consistently be relied
upon to supply it (Butler & Cantrell, 1984; Mishra, 1996). Reliability implies a sense of confidence that you can "rest assured" that
you can count on a person doing what is expected on a regular, consistent basis. You need not invest energy worrying whether the person will come through or make mental provisions of how to manage
in case of failure.

Reliability in Brenda's school often meant demonstrating a willingness to address problems, no matter what it took. This sometimes
meant that Brenda worked long hours to get everything done. Dependability and a high level of commitment were apparently contagious. Kathy described her principal this way: "Brenda is a very
hard worker. She is here every morning at 6:30 and she doesn't go

home until things are done. She may be here until 8 or 9 o'clock in the evening if there are meetings. Seeing her do that, well, the school gives 110 percent. Everybody works hard here."

Sometimes Brenda worked too hard, leading her on occasion to become short-tempered. Her teachers seemed willing to forgive her, recognizing that she had enormous demands made on her. They appreciated her dedication to them and to the school.

Teachers have greater confidence when they feel they can predict the behavior of their principal. For principals to garner the trust of their faculty they need to demonstrate enough consistency in their behavior to inspire confidence that teachers can count on them in their time of need. Consistency between the beliefs a person espouses and school goals, as well as with actual behavior, promotes trust in school leaders (Bryk & Schneider, 2002; Evans, 1996). Teachers commented that it not only increased their trust in their leaders to see them stepping up to the plate in predictable and occasionally extraordinary ways, it also increased their own motivation.

Competence

Good intentions are not always enough. When a person is dependent on another and some level of skill is involved in fulfilling an expectation, an individual who means well may nonetheless not be trusted (Baier, 1994; Mishra, 1996). Competence is the ability to perform a task as expected, according to appropriate standards. In schools, principals and teachers depend upon one another's competence to accomplish the teaching and learning goals of the school. Likewise, students are dependent on the competence of their teachers. A student may feel

A FOUR-FOOT long Ball Python snake escaped from a terrarium in one of the classrooms at our school. Our principal crawled up through the rafters looking for it. She and her husband prowled through the school with a flashlight at midnight until the snake was found. And she hates snakes!

Lynn, special education teacher

that her teacher is benevolent and wishes very much to help her learn, but if the teacher lacks knowledge of the subject matter or cannot adequately communicate that knowledge, the student may lack trust in the teacher. If the lack of skill is evidenced in an apprentice, however, such as a student teacher, it is understood that the person is still learning and expected to make some mistakes, so the lack of competence is not a breach of trust (Solomon & Flores, 2001). In this case, failure should not be confused with betrayal because the person did not claim to have the requisite skill. Presumably the system has safeguards in place to protect others from the harm of the mistakes of an apprentice.

We trust people whose skill we depend upon, especially professionals, to be honest about their level of skill and to maintain their skills. This effort reflects not merely on their reliability but on their character and conscientiousness (Solomon & Flores, 2001). The problem is, however, that people are not always honest with themselves (or sufficiently insightful) about their loss of skills and the impairment of their judgment. A superintendent who is fighting a drinking problem or a teacher who has "retired on the job" and is no longer effective with students raises serious questions of trust. Reputation comes into play as well when it comes to trust based on competence. A new principal to a building, even if she is well intentioned and demonstrates good will, may have difficulty earning the trust of teachers and parents if she is preceded by a reputation of incompetence or ineffectiveness.

Teachers often mention incidents in which the competence of their principal matters. In high-trust schools, principals are regarded with respect and even admiration. In these schools the principals not only set a high standard, they also hold teachers accountable in ways that seem fair and reasonable to their staff. At Brookside School, the faculty was confident that Brenda was on top of things.

Kathy talked about Brenda's competence and what it meant for the school: "Brenda is just very aware of everything in the building. She reads every report card, every conference report. She does recess duty every day, herself with aides, because she wants to be there when the problems happen and stop them. She doesn't want the problems to escalate; she wants to stop them from the minute they start. She is very much an integral part of the school. She *is* the school."

The teachers felt reassured by this level of commitment and involvement from their principal. With caring, came a sense of accountability. Kathy continued: "She rarely takes a sick day, she's always here. She is in every class, everyday between 9 and 9:30. She always wears heels. You can hear those heels clicking in the hall and you know you better put yourself in order. She makes her presence known!"

This level of involvement gave the faculty a sense of confidence that the school was being managed effectively, despite the inevitable difficulties inherent in an urban setting. There was confidence that problems would not be allowed to get out of hand. It is not necessary, or even desirable, that principals have a hand in everything that goes on in their school. But they need to have enough awareness to know when problems are emerging in order to respond to them.

One way that principals demonstrate their competence is in their willingness to buffer teachers and handle difficult situations, whether dealing with difficult students or distressed parents, or discretely handling problems among the faculty and staff. One of a principal's primary responsibilities is to protect the core work of the school—the teaching and learning process. This may mean being the first line of defense in disruptions that come from the outside, such as calming an irate parent who demands to speak to a teacher immediately, or assisting in creating a schoolwide climate that is serious about learning and does not condone student misconduct. Fred lost the confidence of his teachers because of the lack of support they felt in dealing with unruly students. Teachers thought his low-key approach sent the message to students that they could do as they pleased and that no serious consequences were likely to come their way. A calm demeanor in the face of an angry parent or a child who is out of control can be reassuring to a teacher who is upset. The good rapport that Brenda had built with parents helped the teachers at Brookside in their work. Christy reported: "People have a lot of respect for Brenda. She knows the families. We have gone on home visits and she doesn't even have to look up the address. The parents come to her. The parents come back to her after the kids have graduated from Brookside. She is very much into home-school cooperation."

Trust, then, allows a person to rest assured in a situation where something that person cares about depends, at least in part, on another person. That assurance has to do with confidence based on intention and integrity, bolstered by openness, reliability, and competence. Faculty trust in the principal is based on what teachers feel they ought to be able to expect from a person who occupies that role. What teachers seem to expect, above all, is a sense of caring, benevolence, or good will from their principal. Principals who have a reputation for integrity and who encourage open communication are principals who are likely to earn the trust of their teachers. Because they feel vulnerable to the problems that emerge from an incompetent or disengaged principal, teachers also rely heavily on competence as a basis of trust. Principals who are disposed to assist teachers to solve problems in order to help them do their jobs also are more likely to be trusted. Statistical evidence of surveys from a large and diverse sample of schools confirms that all of these facets are important aspects of trust relations in schools (Hoy & Tschannen-Moran, 1999). They are the key ingredients that make for trustworthy leadership (Table 2.1.).

Differentiated Trust

Although all these facets of trust are important, their relative weight will depend on the nature of the interdependence and consequent vulnerability in the relationship. One is vulnerable in different ways to an intimate friend, a boss, an investment broker, or a surgeon.

Table 2.1. Facets of Trust

Facets of Trust	
Benevolence	Caring, extending good will, having positive intentions, supporting teachers, expressing appreciation for staff efforts, being fair, guarding confidential information
Honesty	Having integrity, telling the truth, keeping promises, honoring agreements, having authenticity, accepting responsibility, avoiding manipulation, being real, being true to oneself
Openness	Engaging in open communication, sharing important information, delegating, sharing decision making, sharing power
Reliability	Having consistency, being dependable, demonstrating commitment, having dedication, being diligent
Competence	Setting an example, engaging in problem solving, fostering conflict resolution (rather than avoidance), working hard, pressing for results, setting standards, buffering teachers, handling difficult situations, being flexible

For trust to form, it may not be necessary to have a high level of confidence in all facets, only in those areas in which there is critical interdependence. There are crucial thresholds across which trust turns to distrust. Different facets of trust may have different thresholds depending on the level of reliance in a particular area and the consequences of one's expectations being disappointed (Shaw, 1997). For example, if you are aware that a friend is less than trustworthy in some realm that does not directly concern you, such as that he cheats on his income taxes or is somewhat unreliable in aspects of his work responsibilities, but he is faithful in his dealing with you, you may nonetheless trust him.

As relationships mature, trust evolves from impressionistic and undifferentiated to a more finely grained and differentiated form. As interdependent partners in an ongoing relationship gather experience with one another, they come to have a growing pool of trust-relevant evidence to draw upon. However, the trust picture that emerges may not be a simple one. Trust becomes more differentiated and may be uneven. Relationships are multifaceted; therefore, a person may trust another in some matters and not in others so that trust and distrust may be simultaneously present in the same relationship (Lewicki & Bunker, 1996; Lewicki, et al., 1998). For example, in a situation of two teachers who have taught together for years and have come to have an abiding trust for one another, the relationship of interdependence changes when one of the teachers becomes an assistant principal in the school where they have taught together. The teacher is now vulnerable to her former peer in new ways, as that person takes on greater organizational authority and power. Because the nature of the interdependence has changed, trust must now be reassessed based on the new dimensions of this relationship, especially if the culture of that school emphasizes the differences in orientation between teachers and administrators. This example raises questions of the challenges of establishing trust across the lines of hierarchy, the topic of the next section.

Trust and Hierarchy

Because of the hierarchical nature of the relationships within schools, it is the responsibility of the person with greater power to take the initiative to build and sustain trusting relationships. Because of their greater feelings of vulnerability, subordinates seem to be hypervigilant in their trust assessments of superiors so that even relatively minor gestures take on considerable importance. When subordinate-superior dyads were interviewed about their relationships, subordinates recalled more trust-related incidents than superiors, and trust violations tended to "loom larger" than confirmations of trustworthiness (Kramer, 1996). Because the faculty at Lincoln felt vulnerable to Gloria's whims and did not trust her, they kept a close eye on her moods and actions for clues as to how they might protect themselves.

There are two basic underlying structures of organizations: bureaucratic and professional (Hoy & Miskel, 2001). Bureaucratic organizations rely on a hierarchy of authority for coordination and control, whereas professional organizations rely on trust in the expertise of the professionals to exercise discretion in responding to the needs of clients. Schools are a unique combination of bureaucratic and professional organizations. Although bureaucratic structures often seem to get in the way of productivity, that need not be the case. In productive schools, such as Brookside, principals and teachers are able to work cooperatively across recognized boundaries of authority while retaining their distinctive roles (Hirschhorn, 1997). Teachers feel confident and are able to exercise discretion in their professional roles. Brenda exercised authority in a way that was flexible, cooperative, and collaborative, in contrast to Gloria, who was rigid, autocratic, and controlling. Trustworthy principals help teachers and staff members solve problems rather than get in the way of their work. In productive schools, principals use their power and authority to design structures that facilitate teaching and learning and buffer teachers from needless interruptions and distractions (Hoy & Sweetland, 2000, 2001).

Trust depends, in part, on what one expects of another on the basis of formal roles and informal norms. The reality of life in organizations is that individuals are invested with varying degrees of power and authority. People at different hierarchical levels examine and weigh sources of trust-relevant information differently. They look to one another with divergent expectations of what they owe to others, and about what others owe them. These differential expectations influence the cultivation of trust. In schools, principals base their judgments of trust of teachers more heavily on competence, reliability, and commitment, whereas teachers' views of principals tend to be anchored more in caring, integrity, and openness (Blake & MacNeil, 1998; Spuck & MacNeil, 1999).

Putting It into Action

The behavior of principals plays a critical role in setting the tone of trust within a school. If you hope to benefit from the rewards of a trusting culture, it is your responsibility to initiate trusting relationships through your own trusting and trustworthy behavior (Whitener, Brodt, Korsgaard, & Werner, 1998). Brenda is an excellent example of a trustworthy principal, but her story is in no way unique. She shares many characteristics with other trustworthy principals. Like Brenda, they evidence enormous caring for the teachers, staff, students, and parents in their schools. High performance expectations for all members of the community grow out of this sense of care. Brenda was both consistent and competent. She was known for her integrity. And Brenda inspired trust by being open in communication and control, keeping the faculty, students, and parents of Brookside informed about matters of importance to them and involving them in important decisions. In extending trust, she was trusted in return.

To be a trustworthy principal is first and foremost to be known as a person of good will. Teachers are confident that you have their best interests at heart and will do whatever is possible to help them develop as professionals. The form that this caring takes will vary across schools, but it will be evident that you are strongly committed to the well-being of all of the individuals who make up your school community. You need to protect other's rights and welfare, and refrain from exploiting others in order to advance your own interests. You can promote trust by demonstrating consideration and sensitivity for teachers' needs and interests, listening intently to communicate respect for the person, and engaging in coaching and problem solving if that is what is needed. Making yourself visible and accessible will allow you to more readily demonstrate your support and concern.

To be a trustworthy principal you must be honest and fair in dealings with the faculty, students, and parents. You will need to demonstrate integrity in telling the truth and keeping promises. You will also need to demonstrate authenticity by accepting responsibility for your actions and avoiding distorting the truth in order to shift blame to others. Trust is also enhanced by a willingness to apologize for mistakes or when a decision you have made results in unpleasant consequences for members of the school community (Greenberg, 1993; Konovsky & Pugh, 1994).

As a trustworthy school leader you will want to foster an open flow of information that allows you to be made aware of problems while they are still small. You will foster trust by truly involving teachers in important decisions. It is important that you be consistent, even predictable, not arbitrary or capricious. You will need to model hard work and dedication, be engaged with the faculty, and cultivate awareness of what is going on in your building. By acting in trusting and trustworthy ways, you can create a school that reaps the rewards of a culture of trust.

Key Points About Defining Trust

- Trust is a glue that holds things together, as well as a lubricant that reduces friction and facilitates smooth operations. Trust is also a choice that involves risk.

- In situations of interdependence, when the outcomes you desire rely to some extent on someone else, you want to feel confident that the other person is benevolent, honest, open, reliable, and competent.

- As relationships mature, trust evolves from impressionistic and highly undifferentiated to more finely grained and differentiated among specific facets of trust.

- Because principals have greater power within the relationships in a school, they have greater responsibility for the establishment and maintenance of a culture of trust.

- The principal's behavior has a large influence on the culture of the school. Visible and accessible principals can more readily demonstrate support and concern.

- To be trusted, principals need to be willing to extend trust to teachers, staff, students, and parents.

Questions for Reflection and Discussion

1. How can an understanding of the five facets of trust help bolster the culture of trust in your building?

2. In which facets do you judge yourself to be a trustworthy leader? In which would you like to improve? What disciplines, habits, and techniques can help you focus on the facets of trust during the school day?

3. Can you recall an incident when you felt torn between a need to maintain confidentiality and a desire for openness? How did you handle it? What was the result?

3

Cultivating Trust

Trust is a human virtue, cultivated through speech,
conversation, commitments, and action.
Solomon and Flores (2001)

If trust is good, how then is it established? This is a fundamental question for those who would lead schools in the twenty-first century. The answer is complex. Trust is a multidimensional and dynamic phenomenon. The way trust unfolds will not be the same at all times and in all places. It takes on different characteristics at different stages of a relationship. As trust develops, it "gels" at different levels, depending on the nature of the relationship and the quality of the interactions as parties have gotten to know one another. The nature of vulnerability can change as the level of interdependence increases or decreases and as expectations are either met or disappointed. Initially, trust relies on assumptions, institutional structures, and deterrents. With greater history of expectations being met, as well as the growth of a sense of caring about the relationship, trust may deepen. Understanding the developmental nuances of trust is an essential prerequisite for leaders who want to foster and maintain trust in their schools.

Initial Trust

Organizations exist to accomplish tasks that are too big, complex, and costly for individuals alone to accomplish. When a new member joins an organization, a level of interdependence is initiated immediately by virtue of the shared purpose embodied by the organization. A new employee's success and continued employment depends on the ability to forge workable relationships with the existing organizational players and to serve organizational purposes. When Christy was hired at Brookside, she joined an already established school community with its own history, culture, and norms. Her developing trust was facilitated by the feeling of camaraderie and good humor evident at the school. As Gloria assumed leadership of Lincoln School, she joined an ongoing operation, with a particular history and with certain expectations and goals for what would be accomplished under her leadership. Her actions were scrutinized by the existing members of the school community for clues as to whether they could trust her or not.

As trust develops in newly forming work relationships, an initial period of impression making is followed by a period of more intense exploration. Trust is established through a commitment period during which each partner has the opportunity to signal to the other a willingness to accept personal risk and not to exploit the vulnerability of the other for personal gain. A kind of courtship takes place in which each party is careful not to violate the other's developing trust (Shapiro, Sheppard, & Cheraskin, 1992). This commitment period begins at the moment of initial contact and extends until participants know each other well enough to predict one another's values and behavior. As participants begin to feel more comfortable with one another, there may be a tacit testing of the limits of trust and influence and attempts to arrive at a mutual set of expectations. Within eighteen months, relationships generally become fairly stable (Gabarro, 1978).

When Gloria became principal at Lincoln, her actions during the commitment period signaled to the faculty and staff that they ought to be wary in their relationship with her. Because of the pressure she felt to make change quickly, she did not invest the time to develop the requisite trust needed to lead people through change. Although it was clear she had been hired to turn around a failing school, her impatience for change was perceived as disrespectful by those who had invested their professional lives at Lincoln. The relationships had soured before the end of the first year, and stabilized at a point of suspicion and distrust. From there, it was hard to make reparations and to reestablish productive working relationships.

Although it makes intuitive sense that trust grows gradually over time, researchers have been surprised to find higher levels of initial trust than expected, even though the parties have very little knowledge or experience of one another. It seems that when people interact with a stranger, they tend to extend a provisional trust until evidence surfaces to suggest that the other is untrustworthy, thus making defensive action necessary. This preference for provisional trust over initial distrust makes sense because trust is the easier option. Distrust requires that energy be expended in anticipating possible harm and in planning ways to avert it (Berg, Dickhaut, & McCabe, 1995; Jones & George, 1998). People are

---

I WORKED FOR a man with whom I had a great deal of trust. Before we even met, I knew of his reputation for the good things he did in the community. From our very first meeting, he treated me like a colleague. He treated me with respect. At one of our first meetings, he challenged an assertion I made. I reinforced my point. We went back and forth several times on the point, but he never pulled rank or insisted that I agree with his interpretation just because he had greater power. That was the basis of a strong working relationship over time.

Janine, music educator

inclined to overlook the possibility that the other person may not share their values and consequently will fail to meet their expectations in the relationship. As individuals interact, experience either reinforces these trusting assumptions or dispels initial impressions of trustworthiness. Once people have evidence that leads them to perceive differences in values, distrust is likely to emerge (Sitkin & Roth, 1993).

Institutional Supports

High initial trust in organizations such as schools is a function of not just the efficiency of assumed trustworthiness but also of the institutional mechanisms, such as policies, rules, and regulations, that support trust. The belief that the necessary organizational structures are in place to allow one to anticipate a successful interchange and the outcome one desires can support the development of initial trust (McKnight, Cummings, & Chervany, 1998; Shapiro, 1987; Zucker, 1986). Formal organizational policies and informal social structures such as the norms and values of the culture support developing trust (Creed & Miles, 1996). These factors can also sustain a cycle of risk taking and fulfillment that facilitates the deepening of trust (Gulati, 1995; Sitkin, 1995).

The mechanisms involved in the hiring process are key institutional supports for initial trust. Schools cannot afford to be naive concerning trust when hiring new members because a failure to detect untrustworthiness is a breach of the trust that parents and taxpayers have placed in the system. The hiring process is an intentional process of gathering trust-relevant information on both sides of the hiring decision. From the first contact with a prospective employee, schools not only gather information about the person's background and check with references who have knowledge of the person, they also pay special attention to the character of the interactions to be sure they do not sense anything out of the ordinary. Likewise, the prospective employee is judging the feel of the place and is trying to pick up any discrepancies between what is said and what is done. A general impression or an intuitive sense that everything "feels normal" supports initial trust (McKnight et al., 1998). If both sides successfully establish an initial level of trust, the person may join the organization. Organizational participants interacting with a new employee may feel at ease in extending initial trust, assuming that the proper procedures are in place to root out evidence of untrustworthiness.

Another of the institutional supports to trust in schools is the certification of teachers and administrators. The premise is that a professional must demonstrate a certain level of competence and knowledge to receive certification and is consequently qualified for his or her position. Reliability is addressed to some extent in the contract that spells out the job description and expectations. The other facets of trust, benevolence, honesty, and openness, are not as readily supported by institutional mechanisms but may be supported by the norms of the school or school district because a person violating those norms will risk reaping sanctions and social disapproval (Baier, 1994).

Reputation

In the early stages of a relationship, as people get to know one another, they rely on the reputation of others to guide them in assuming an initial level of trust. This is especially true for educational leaders who live out their careers in the public eye. A reputation of trustworthiness is a valuable asset to individuals and organizations alike, and can become a self-fulfilling prophesy. When Christy applied to transfer to Brookside, it was in part because of Brenda's reputation for excellence and trustworthiness. She knew that she would be expected to work harder than teachers at most other schools in the district, but she also felt confident that she would be treated as a professional. Once she joined the faculty, the stories that she heard from other teachers about Brenda served to enhance her developing trust.

The trust between two individuals is significantly influenced by the social context in which that relationship is embedded. A network of mutual friends and acquaintances can enhance the likelihood that a trusting relationship will develop and strengthen trust as it develops; however, such a context can also amplify the effects of a breach of trust. The judgment, observations, and gossip of others can tend to "lock in" relationships at either positive or negative extremes (Burt & Knez, 1996). Stories that are told and retold through the school's grapevine serve to further a cycle of either trust or distrust. The stories that circulated at Brookside built trust in Brenda and sustained trust despite an occasional lapse on Brenda's part, whereas the stories told about Gloria reinforced the sense of violation that certain teachers felt, which spread to others who had not been directly affected.

Because trust is only relevant in the context of interdependence and vulnerability, individuals tend to be more alert to negative information and prefer negative gossip to positive. This can be an impediment to the development of trust. Technologies, such as e-mail, voice mail, and the Internet, allow gossip to spread more quickly and can amplify the impact of broken trust. In addition, misunderstandings introduced in the abbreviated forms of communication often employed in e-mail and instant messaging can cause the disruption of trust. The propensity of the news media to capitalize on the desire for negative information has made the cultivation of trust more difficult between schools and their publics.

Relationships within schools tend to be ongoing in that people expect to continue to relate to the same network of people over time. Because of this, the social network can exert both formal and informal control that encourages people to act in a trustworthy manner. There is an incentive to behave in ways that are trustworthy, develop a reputation for trustworthiness, and reap the benefits of trusting relationships (Coleman, 1990; Fukuyama, 1995; Putnam, 1993). When many people perceive that an individual has a good reputation, it is more difficult for a negative event to significantly reduce a high level of trust in that individual (McKnight et al., 1998).

Factors That Influence Developing Trust

School leaders need to understand that a number of factors come into play as trust develops. Trust judgments can be influenced by one's disposition to trust, by values and attitudes, and by moods and emotions, especially attitudes concerning diversity. The role that each of these factors plays in the development of trust is explored next.

Disposition to Trust

Some people are inclined to extend trust more readily; they have a disposition to trust. A disposition to trust is particularly pertinent to making trust judgments when people do not know each other and specific information about the other person is not available. A person's disposition toward trust may stem from a person's history of relationships, in which promises have either been fulfilled or broken. A child whose upbringing was consistent may develop a generally trusting disposition, whereas a child who has been regularly disappointed by broken promises or a lack of good will may grow up with a generalized suspicion of people's motives and promises. These early expectations may then generalize from one societal actor to another, such as from one's parents to teachers, the media, or the government. A person with a high disposition to trust is more likely to see good points and to overlook flaws in another person that could threaten the development of trust (Johnson-George & Swap, 1982; Rotter, 1980).

A person with a disposition to trust is likely to have both a faith in humanity and a trusting stance. Faith in humanity has to do with believing that others are typically well-meaning and reliable. A trusting stance, however, is one that treats people as though they are reliable and trustworthy despite an absence of evidence, based on the belief that this strategy more often than not results in more positive outcomes (McKnight et al., 1998; Solomon & Flores, 2001). In the absence of contrary data, extending trust may be the wisest course in establishing a relationship. People with a trusting disposition tend to be more trustworthy than others; they are less likely to lie, cheat, or steal, even when they can increase their gain by being untrustworthy. In general, high trusters seem to be happier, more popular, and considered a better friend than those with low-trusting dispositions. They are less likely to be conflicted, maladjusted, or dependent on others (Deutsch, 1960; Rotter, 1967; Wrightsman, 1966).

There is an important distinction between trust, naiveté, and blind trust. Naïveté is inattention to trust-relevant information, a taking for granted of the dynamic process that forms the basis for cultivating a trusting relationship. People with a disposition to trust are not necessarily more gullible or naive; they are able to make use of information about the behavior of others in given situations to guide their actions regardless of their disposition toward trust. For example, high trusters may be more likely to be cooperative initially, but they do not continue to trust once they have been tricked (Schlenker, Helm, & Tedeschi, 1973). Blind trust, however, is not really trust but willful self-deception. It is refusal to take stock of the evidence of untrustworthy behavior or to take measures of self-protection. Giving second chances even when one has been let down may not be blind trust when one willingly acknowledges the disappointment of trust (Solomon & Flores, 2001). For example, when a principal catches a new teacher telling a half-truth in covering up for some mistake but gives the teacher another chance, it is not blind trust if she acknowledges the disappointment. Blind trust is active denial of the evidence by refusing to acknowledge even the possibility of betrayal.

Values and Attitudes

People make trust judgments in part on the basis of the assumption of shared values. Values are general standards or principles that are considered intrinsically desirable ends, such as loyalty, helpfulness, or fairness. Attitudes are knowledge structures consisting of the thoughts and feelings individuals have about other people, groups, or organizations. They are the means through which interactions are defined and structured. Attitudes are evaluative in nature, and values are a key means people use to evaluate others (Jones & George, 1998). Because relationships within organizations involve interdependence and a certain amount of uncertainty, people form attitudes toward each other that are likely to contain information about the other party's trustworthiness based on perceptions of shared values. For example, a teacher who had been hired at Fremont was distrusted by some because of the harsh and demeaning tone she took with her students, as she was overheard from the hallway. A teacher who had worked at Brookside the previous year was perceived not to have the same work ethic as the rest of the faculty and so was perceived not to share the same values about the importance and urgency of the work to be done. That teacher was counseled into transferring to another school at the end of the year.

Distrust can arise in a school when an individual or group is perceived as not sharing key cultural values. When a person challenges a school's fundamental assumptions and values, that person may be perceived as operating under values so different from the group's that the violator's underlying world view becomes suspect. Threat of future violations arises because the person is now seen as a cultural outsider, one who "doesn't think like us" who may, therefore, do the "unthinkable" (Sitkin & Roth, 1993). Some schools' values, however, may be appropriately called into question. There may be a legitimate basis for people to be skeptical about whether the schools' aims are legitimate and whether they are doing what they are supposed to be doing. Gloria had reason to question the underlying values and assumptions about students that accepted low achievement at Lincoln, based on the reputation for poor student performance. Pointed questioning might be very appropriate and might be quite useful to get the organization to focus more clearly on its legitimate core values. What was missed in Gloria's rush to assert that low student performance would no longer be tolerated was the fostering of relationships and a context for that conversation that would make it constructive. It takes time to build a productive culture that deals effectively with conflict, encourages open dialogue, and even dissent.

People have a tendency to extend trust more readily to those they perceive as similar to themselves based on the assumption that they have adopted similar norms of obligation and cooperation learned through similar cultural structures (Zucker, 1986). The perceived similarity may be based on characteristics such as family background, social status, or ethnicity. One of the dynamics that contributed to a lack of effectiveness at Fremont was racial tension among the faculty. Many of the African American teachers had gone to school together, belonged to the same sorority, and attended the same large church. This group had a long history with one another and shared strong bonds of friendship. They were very involved in each others' lives outside of school and shared many inside jokes. These teachers made a big deal of celebrating one another's birthdays, with catered lunches, cake, and balloons. The white teachers were not invited to attend these celebrations. Fred's attendance at these affairs was taken as a tacit acceptance of these divisions, which to some white teachers felt like a betrayal. This group was perceived to be very cliquish by many of the white teachers. If any of the members ever felt slighted by or were in conflict with someone outside the group, the outsider was likely to experience the wrath of the whole group. The teachers in this group felt comfortable extending trust to one another more readily than to others because they could be assumed to have adopted similar norms of obligation and cooperation through the cultural structures of school, sorority, and church.

Trust is more difficult in situations of diversity because people are uncertain about the cultural norms or values of others (Kipnis, 1996). Knowledge of one another's culture may be limited and based on partial or misleading images. Hence, people are often unsure about what to expect. To simplify the complexity of relationships, people tend to divide others into two groups: those with whom they share group membership and those who are outside that group. Once others have been categorized, people make biased assumptions, based on group membership, about the others' values, preferences, behavior, and trustworthiness. People are more likely to regard out-group members with suspicion and to stereotype them more readily and negatively than in-group members. Biased attributions about the capabilities, intentions, and actions of out-group members can fuel feelings of distrust. Individuals tend to attribute the motivations for the behavior of out-group members to differences in underlying attitudes or values, whereas with in-group members they are more likely to consider situational factors that might have influenced behavior (Allison & Messick, 1985). Thus, an African American teacher who made an inappropriate remark might be excused by other members of the clique as just having a bad day, whereas the same remark from a white teacher might be seen as evidence of bigotry or poor moral character. Furthermore, people are more likely to seek information that conforms to their attitudes about their own and other groups and to discount information that disconfirms their biases (Klayman & Ha, 1997).

Group biases can be destructive not only by causing people to regard out-group members

As African Americans we learn early that Caucasians are not to be trusted. Consequently, we are always waiting for the other shoe to drop in our professional and personal relationships. The history of poor race relations makes trust very difficult.

Melody, special educator

with suspicion but also by promoting too much trust for in-group members. Members develop a "leniency-bias" for those of the in-group, giving other in-group members the benefit of the doubt when confronted with information that might otherwise be viewed as diagnostic of untrustworthiness (Brewer, 1995). Overconfidence in the collective can lead individuals to "defer too readily to other members, and may inhibit expressions of doubt, or engage in inappropriately severe self-censorship rather than press their claims as vigorously as they might" (Kramer et al., 1996, p. 381). A strong, cohesive culture that perceives itself under threat and so stifles dissent can result in "groupthink," a dynamic that has been exposed as a factor in some disastrously poor decisions (Janis, 1982).

Trust judgments based on similarity or group membership can have very real consequences for how schools function. For example, in one study, superiors expressed less trust and were less willing to use participative approaches in decision making for subordinates who were predominately from a minority group (Rosen & Jerdee, 1977). But research on teachers' trust of students and parents has indicated that socioeconomic status was a stronger dividing line for differentiating in- and out-group perceptions than race (Tschannen-Moran, 2001). Schools face increasing diversity of languages, ethnic groups, races, and socioeconomic status. This diversity brings a richness, but it also brings challenges for the development of trust. Diverse groups need time, structure, and support to learn about one another and to come to view themselves as part of the same collective. They need knowledge of one another's culture and values so they can come to be able to predict behavior and

I WAS BROUGHT UP to respect everyone. There are times when I have been the victim of racial prejudice, but I choose not to dwell on it. I have a good relationship with everyone in my school—they trust me and I trust them. They respect me, because as a black man I can get through to some of the kids that the white teachers can't. To me, trust begins with respect.

Howard, elementary school head custodian

have confidence that expectations will be met. Diversity can present an especially daunting challenge to the development of trust when the exploration of cultural differences reveals very real differences in values.

Moods and Emotions

Although trust is not a feeling, moods and emotions do provide a powerful context for trust judgments. Emotions are intense affective states tied to particular events or circumstances that interrupt ongoing cognitive processes and behaviors, whereas moods are less intense, generalized affective states that are not explicitly linked to particular events or circumstances. Anger is an emotion likely to emerge in response to betrayal, one that intrudes upon one's thoughts and may be accompanied by physiological changes such as a flushed face or clinched jaw and fists. A mood of cynicism may emerge after a series of disappointments leads to diminished hope that the situation is likely to improve.

Moods are our way of being "tuned" into the world. They are more akin to a habit of mind than to something that comes over people and over which they have no control. Moods are not just occasional occurrences: we are always in a mood. Our moods do not simply "happen" to us. We cultivate our moods through our thoughts and practices. Moods are not simply an emotional response to what has happened, but an orientation toward the future—about what is to be done (Jones & George, 1998; Solomon & Flores, 2001). There are many variations of being in a "bad mood":

- Resignation ("Nothing is going to improve this situation, and there is nothing I can do to change it.")

- Despair ("Nothing can prevent this looming calamity. We might as well just let it happen.")

- Distrust ("I don't believe what they told me, so I'm certainly not going to put my heart into it.")

- Cynicism ("Nothing ever changes, and nothing ever gets better, so it is silly even to try.")

- Confusion ("I don't know what's going on here and I don't know who to ask, and I can't afford to let anyone know that I don't know what I'm doing.")

- Panic ("I'll never be able to do this!")

- Resentment, the most devastating of all bad moods ("My colleagues don't ever give me the respect I deserve.") (Solomon & Flores, 2001, pp. 110–111)

Just as people's orientations toward the world are shaped by moods, organizational cultures might be likened to moods. Low morale can be thought of as the organization's being in a "bad mood." When a culture or mood of resignation is pervasive in a school, it functions as a self-protective mechanism that steels participants against the possibility of further disappointment. In an attempt to avoid disappointment, people refrain from taking any assertive action. They close off the possibilities of negotiation and mutual understanding that might lead to an improved relationship. When people have lost their grip on hope so that resignation reaches a point of despair, taking preventive action ceases to make sense (Solomon & Flores, 2001).

There are times when an organization adopts a culture of "cordial hypocrisy" that appears on the surface as a good mood, but when probed turns out to be a cover for a more deeply pervasive culture of despair, resignation, or resentment. At its worst this veneer of courtesy and amiability is a collective form of self-deception and denial, and thus is immune to easy resolution (Solomon & Flores, 2001). Cordial hypocrisy is evident in schools that suppress conflict rather than create constructive mechanisms for its resolution (Uline, Tschannen-Moran, & Perez, 2003). A healthy school climate is one in which conflict is seen as a natural and even helpful part of schools and is harnessed for school improvement.

Once moods are recognized as self-chosen and culturally endorsed ways of being in the organization and the world, the way is open to change them. Solomon and Flores (2001) explain the vital role that conversation plays in changing organizational cultures. "The key to cultivating [better] moods is the revision of these assessments: understanding through conversation just how others see the situation and, just as important, how they see you and your role in the situation. Conversation leads to mutual understanding, and understanding should lead to resolutions and engagements, actions that will bring about new situations and open up new possibilities" (p. 113).

Schools, like individuals, do not need to be trapped by their bad moods. With understanding and effort, those negative habits of mind can be turned to a more constructive orientation about "what is to be done." School leaders who want to cultivate a culture of trust will be aided by an understanding of how trust develops and the factors that can facilitate or hamper its growth.

Authentic and Optimal Trust

Trustworthy leaders assist their schools to develop authentic and optimal levels of trust. Authentic trust emerges when people have grown to have a deep and abiding trust in one another. Each relies on the other in a full and complete way, resting in interdependence and vulnerability without anxiety. There is empathy with the other party's desires and intentions, and mutual understanding such that each can effectively act on the other's behalf (Jones & George, 1998; Lewicki & Bunker, 1996).

Trust deepens and becomes more authentic as individuals interact and get to know one another over time (Zucker, 1986). Relationships mature as the frequency and duration of interactions increase and with the diversity of challenges that relationship partners face together. The more experience parties have, the better the chances they will come to understand and be able to predict each others' behavior (Lewicki & Bunker, 1996). Reliability in previous interactions gives rise to positive expectations that goodwill will be returned in kind (Creed & Miles, 1996). A self-reinforcing pattern of trust emerges as repeated cycles of exchange, risk taking, and successful fulfillment of expectations strengthen the willingness of trusting parties to rely upon each other. A history of fulfilled expectations accumulates and leads to a reputation for trustworthiness that can then facilitate and reinforce trust in a wider social context.

An abiding, authentic trust is also a robust trust that can endure an occasional disappointment, disagreement, or difference in values provided it leaves intact the sense of both parties caring enough to protect and continue the relationship. Trust can rebound, particularly if both parties make an effort to restore a sense of good faith and fair dealing in their interactions (Rousseau et al., 1998). Each can recognize that the other is human and bound to err and nonetheless make the decision to go on trusting (Solomon & Flores, 2001).

Some have labeled this abiding trust "unconditional trust"; however, trust is almost always bounded and specific (Solomon & Flores, 2001). Trust is limited to the context and capacity expected of the other person. For example, a trusted colleague at work would not necessarily be trusted with one's prized sailboat if he or she did not have the skill to operate it properly. A trusted spouse would not necessarily be trusted to perform a medical procedure he or she was not trained to do. At Brookside, the teachers held a deep authentic trust for Brenda and identified with her vision for the school. This relationship of trust even extended beyond the bounds of professional life, as Brenda was relied upon for advice and assistance in personal matters. But even here, there were limits or boundaries to the trust.

So what is the optimal level of trust? More trust is not always better. There are dangers in both trusting too little and trusting too much. Trusting too little is undesirable because schools miss out on the potential of trust to confer a competitive advantage through greater adaptability, lowered costs, and reduced uncertainty (Barney & Hansen, 1994; Mishra, 1996). Too little trust can also be dangerous because one's trust attitudes can be a self-fulfilling prophecy. Organizational participants may begin to live down to the low expectations held for them. Resentment at being treated with the distrust implicit in many bureaucratic regulations can leave workers feeling that if they are already presumed guilty, there is, in fact, little reason to be trustworthy (Fox, 1974).

Yet trusting too much can leave open too wide the gates of temptation. It provides too few incentives to deter workers' inclinations toward opportunism or "looking out for Number One" (Wicks, Berman, & Jones, 1999). This could be seen in the poor citizenship of some of the teachers at Fremont who took advantage of Fred's trust of them to do the right thing and make decisions in the best interest of the school and the students. The lack of constraints tempted these teachers to cut corners on their obligations, lighten their teaching responsibilities, and shorten their workday.

Discerning the proper level of trust requires wisdom and discernment on the part of the educational leader. Optimal trust is prudent, measured, and conditional. Members of the school community need to know not only when to trust others, and in what respects, but also when to monitor others closely (Lewicki et al., 1998). A good model for optimal trust is Aristotle's "golden mean" between excess and deficiency. Trust levels should be appropriate to the context and may fall anywhere on the spectrum from minimal trust to high trust depending on the person and situation (Wicks et al., 1999). Trust needs to be tempered by a willingness to confront and punish exploitive behavior. A bias toward trust shaped by prudence offers an appropriate balance for relationships within school (Solomon & Flores, 2001).

Putting It into Action

As you assume leadership of a new school community, keep in mind that the first few weeks and months are an important phase in the process of developing trust with important stakeholders in the school. You begin the exploration of trust the moment you begin discussions about assuming the leadership of a school building. The hiring process itself is one of gathering trust-relevant information, and the offer of an employment contract speaks to the establishment of a certain level of trust. Your trust relationship with teachers, staff, parents, and even students may begin before any actual contact is made, if your reputation precedes you and as information is disseminated about your having been named to take the leadership of a school.

During the commitment or courtship period, each party has the opportunity to signal a willingness to extend trust and not to exploit the vulnerability of the other. Even if trust is not readily extended to you, it is important to remember that the responsibility for establishing trust rests most heavily with the one with the most power. Because teachers, staff, parents, and students are vulnerable to you, they are going to be watching you closely to discern whether it is safe to trust you. Even small gestures are going to be read as significant as these stakeholders gather information about your trustworthiness.

Fostering trust may be more difficult if you are entering a building where trust is low or where the previous school leader was not perceived as being trustworthy. The faculty and staff may have become jaded by a multiplicity of factors, including failure of past administrators to support them in their work. It is important to recognize that those individuals come by their wariness honestly. Rather than taking their suspicion personally, it will be important for you to be patient and persistent in earning their trust.

Earning trust begins with your willingness to extend trust to the individuals in the school, not blind or naive trust but as much trust as can be reasonably justified based on what you know. A bias toward trust or a trusting stance assumes that the outcomes will be better if you assume people are trustworthy; by extending trust you may be able to provoke more trustworthy behavior on the part of others than if you approach them with suspicion. You will have to discern the appropriate and prudent level of trust, based on the maturity and history of the group as you find it. Trustworthy behavior on your part can cultivate trustworthy norms of behavior among the faculty, staff, and students. In fact, one of the most powerful things that a school leader can do in their first year on the job is to articulate and enforce norms of behavior that will foster a greater level of trust within the school community. Enforcing the norms means calling people who break those norms to account for their actions, doing so in ways that do not embarrass, humiliate, or demean them but that challenge them to better behavior in the future.

Because your actions are going to be scrutinized and mined for meaning as to your intentions and character, be thoughtful about choosing actions that send a message that you want to have received. The first year is not a time to make large, unilateral structural changes, except perhaps to create a mechanism for others to have input into decision making if one does not already exist. Make changes that are symbolic in nature and that communicate your commitment to teachers as well as students and their families. Think about the message that is sent by the entrance to your school. If it doesn't send a positive message, redecorate to send the message that student learning is at the center of what we do here, parents are our partners in this endeavor, and that excellence is achieved through the caring, dedication, and diligence of our teachers. If the teachers' lounge is a dingy, dismal place, offer to raise the funds and enlist parent volunteers to refurbish it (under the direction of the teachers, of course!). Stock it up periodically with good snacks, fresh flowers, or a better grade of coffee.

Find ways—both large and small—to communicate your goodwill and caring toward each member of the school community. Be ready to affirm evidence, even glimmers, of excellence from all corners of the school community. But always be sincere in your thanks and praise; even young children can sense a gratuitous compliment. Small expressions of appreciation for extra effort or good citizenship, a kind word or a brief note, can go a long way toward fueling the motivation for more of the same. Be reliable in following up on the concerns that are brought to you. Carry a notepad and write them down if you need to. Make sure that you are good to your word. Be truthful, even if the truth is, "I don't know, I'll try to find out" or "I can't share that information with you." Be as open with information and control as you feel you can afford to be. And demonstrate your expertise by helping members of the school community solve the problems they encounter in getting their work done. It won't be easy because the demands on school leaders are complex and at times intense. But the trust you earn will facilitate whatever you hope to accomplish through your leadership at the school.

One exercise to assist with the development and maintenance of genuine caring uses what Tim Gallwey calls "the STOP tool" (Gallwey, 2000). Gallwey uses "STOP" as an acronym for step back, think, organize your thoughts, and proceed. He suggests that effective leaders get in the habit of taking daily short STOPs as well as weekly and monthly long STOPs. There is no doubt that school leaders often function at a whirlwind pace that leaves little time for reflection and planning. But trustworthy leaders make the time. They understand reflection as part of their job description, not as an optional extra. Whether it's the first thing they do when they walk in the building or something they practice at another time during the day, the STOP tool can be a useful discipline for educational leaders. Trustworthy leaders use their capacity for critical thinking, visualization, reflective writing, intuition, and humor to guide and improve their management of time, resources, politics, and energy.

Key Points About Cultivating Trust

- In the early stages of developing trust, the reputation of the school and its people plays an important role, but personal factors such as disposition to trust, values, attitudes, moods, and emotions also influence the relationship.

- High trust in educators is supported by formal mechanisms such as certification, job qualifications, hiring procedures, contracts, and rules, as well as the informal mechanisms of norms, values, and a school culture that supports cooperation.

- Trust takes root as participants gain experience and become able to predict how others are likely to behave in a given situation and as they develop a sense of caring for one another and the relationship.

- As trust develops, it "gels" at different levels, depending on the degree of interdependence, knowledge, and experience.

- Authentic trust emerges when the parties have a deep and robust trust in each other, one that can endure an occasional disappointment or difference.

- Optimal trust is a balancing act, as there are dangers in trusting too much as well as in trusting too little.

Questions for Reflection and Discussion

1. What actions did you take when you first arrived at your school building, and how were they received? Was there a mismatch between what you intended and what people perceived? How has trust developed, or failed to develop, over time?

2. If you have missed the "golden mean" of optimal trust, have you tended to trust too much or trust too little? What have been the consequences?

3. How has lack of knowledge of one another's culture created challenges for the development of trust in your school?

4. What is the mood in your school building? Is it productive or does it get in the way of achieving school goals? How might conversation heighten awareness of this habit of mind or orientation toward "what is to be done"?

4

Betrayal

What loneliness is more lonely than distrust?
                                        George Eliot

Situations that entail placing something we care about in the control of another person are situations that require trust. To some extent at least, the outcomes we hope for are determined by someone else. To trust in such circumstances means that we can rest assured in the confidence that things will turn out all right. But what if they don't? What if our expectations are not met? What if the person we have trusted acts carelessly or takes advantage of our confidence for his or her own gain? Situations inevitably arise when what is cared for is harmed, even if by accident, or the trusted person betrays the trust and exploits the other to his or her own advantage.

Trust in relationships is dynamic, in that it can be altered instantaneously with a comment, a betrayed confidence, or a decision that violates the sense of care one has expected of another. When a violation occurs, trust can be shattered, leaving distrust and suspicion in its place (Burt & Knez, 1996). The initial reaction to a violation of trust is often stunned disbelief as the victim begins to come to terms with the breach in expectations. Victims report feeling confused and being left with a sense of unreality. Upon reflection, those feelings often turn to anger and the desire for revenge (Bies & Tripp, 1996).

Betrayals are possible in every realm of life. The focus here is on how betrayal plays out within schools and school districts and on what trustworthy school leaders can do to manage, mediate, and mend these betrayals. The culture and norms of a school or district can influence the likelihood that betrayals will occur. Organizational norms that emphasize ethical behaviors and a work environment of openness, trust, and respect discourage the violation of trust, whereas organizations characterized by negative internal politics, conflict over goals, and shifting coalitions lend themselves to a greater number of betrayals. The culture and norms within a school may not always coincide with the personal expectations of an employee, thus causing intrapersonal as well as interpersonal conflict. For example, Brian, a young teacher at Fremont, thought it was important to abide by contractual standards for staying until a specified time at the end of the school day and experienced both internal and external conflict over the norms at the school that allowed people to slip away soon after the students were dismissed.

The Anatomy of a Betrayal

Betrayal is defined as a voluntary violation of mutually understood expectations that has the potential to threaten the well-being of the trusting person (Elangovan & Shapiro, 1998). Betrayal involves an action or behavior; to constitute a betrayal there needs to be an actual violation rather than just the thought or idea of betraying. An act of betrayal has the potential to cause harm to the trusting person, even if other factors mitigate the actual harm experienced. And even if the violation is not detected by the trusting person, it still constitutes a betrayal. For example, a betrayal occurs when someone reveals potentially damaging information that was shared in confidence, even if the trusting party never learns that his secret has been shared.

In betrayal, the perpetrator makes a choice to violate the expectations of the trusting party, because he or she lacks the motivation to conform to the expectations of the other or becomes motivated to violate these expectations. The motivation to betray results from dissatisfaction with the current situation such that the person believes there is more to be gained than lost by betraying the other person's expectations. Unhappiness with the current situation increases the likelihood of betrayal by lowering the benevolence and integrity of the trusted person. A drop in benevolence implies that the trusted person cares less for the good of the other and may be willing to engage in behaviors that might cause him or her harm. Similarly, a drop in integrity implies that the trusted one is less committed to principles acceptable to the other and may search for justification to switch to an alternate set of principles, even if it means harming the other's best interests. People don't generally like to think of themselves as bad people with poor morals, so they find a way to justify their behavior, at least to themselves, with the hope that they will never be put in the position of having to reveal this (potentially flimsy) rationalization to others. This is followed by a decrease in openness, as the betrayer seeks to avoid detection. The need to be perpetually watchful of one's words and actions can be as damaging to the ongoing relationship as the actual act of betrayal (see Figure 4.1).

In schools, betrayals can be classified as stemming from two broad categories: damage to the civic order or damage to one's sense of identity (Bies & Tripp, 1996). Violations of trust that result in a damaged sense of civic order involve a breech of rules or norms governing behavior and expectations of what people owe to one another in a relationship. These include honor violations such as broken promises, lying, or stealing ideas or credit from others. It could also include shirking of job responsibilities or changing the rules "after the fact." A damaged sense of civic order could also result from the abusive exercise of authority, such as coercive or threatening behavior, improper dismissal, favoritism, and sexual

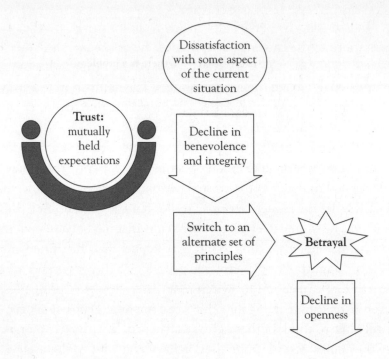

Figure 4.1. The Dynamics of Betrayal

harassment (Harris, 1994). In addition, trust can be damaged by the disclosure of private confidences and secrets. Whereas Fred violated the trust of his faculty mainly through shirking job responsibilities, breaking promises, and stealing credit from others, Gloria committed betrayals through violations involving abusive authority, favoritism, and the manipulative use of job assignments.

The second category of violations of trust involves a sense of damaged identity. A damaged identity can result from public criticism, wrong or unfair accusations, blaming of employees for personal mistakes, or insults to one's self or the collective of which one is a part. When a person's dignity has been damaged, he or she often feels duty bound to redress the wrong and may invest enormous energy in conjuring up a plan to do so. White teachers at Fremont felt betrayed by Fred's tacit approval of the exclusionary practices of the African American teachers on the faculty. At Lincoln, Gloria's numerous insults, both explicit and implicit, of her teachers' professionalism, capability, and commitment, as well as her habit of apportioning blame to her faculty for personal mistakes, left teachers feeling wounded and betrayed.

> OUR PRINCIPAL IS all about blame. If there is a problem, she has to establish that it is someone's fault other than her own before she can begin to solve the problem.
>
> *Michelle, high school teacher*

Whatever its cause, betrayal disrupts trust and damages relationships. The effects of betrayal can be lasting. People generally do not forget even if they forgive and find a way to move on. In a study focusing on betrayal in the workplace, 50 percent of the incidents recounted by participants had occurred more than twenty years earlier, and 25 percent had occurred more than thirty years before (Jones & Burdette, 1994).

Although betrayal involves a violation of personal trust, it is not necessarily unethical or antisocial. A trusted colleague may be put in a situation in which he or she has to choose between betraying a colleague and violating personal principals or organizational norms. For example, if a teacher learns that a friend and colleague has been skimming school fundraising proceeds or has engaged in inappropriate romantic dealings with a student, disclosing this information to the administration would constitute a betrayal of the coworker but could be based on the ethical principles of the informant (Elangovan & Shapiro, 1998).

Conflict is an inevitable part not only of life but of life together at school. It is important not to confuse all conflict with betrayal. School change and school reform are fraught with conflict, as disagreements inevitably arise as to the best course of action, as well as to the pace and order of change (Fullan, 2003). In addition, some people are advantaged by the changes, whereas others may lose favored positions of power. When handled constructively conflict does not necessarily constitute a betrayal, but when handled poorly conflict often results in damaged trust (Uline et al., 2003).

Conflict, like leadership, has two dimensions: commitment to the relationship and commitment to the task (Thomas, 1976). People who are unskilled in conflict resolution tend to handle conflict with a "fight or flight" response. A fight response implies a strong commitment to that task or the goal to be accomplished, and a flight response implies little commitment to the task or goal, but both are low on the relationship dimension. Gloria, on the one hand, demonstrated a fight response to conflict by sacrificing her relationships with teachers in the interests of "winning" her version of reform. Fred, on the other hand, demonstrated the flight response by giving up on both the relationships and the task of school improvement in the interests of avoiding conflict. In so doing, he abdicated his responsibility to both the students and the teachers. Fullan (2003) asserts that "conflict avoidance is an act of moral neglect" (p. 32).

The problem with these fight or flight responses is that both extremes tend to do damage to the trust in a relationship. The fight response demonstrates a willingness to bring harm to the other in

---

I USED TO love my teaching job. I was good friends with my principal and had several close friends on the faculty. All that changed though. Last spring, a few days before our state testing, one of the teachers on my team told me that he had opened the sealed writing prompt in order to give some similar prompts to his students for practice. He offered to share it with me too. I declined, but one other teacher on our team did look over the prompt. At first I kept quiet, but then I just felt heartsick. My conscience was eating away at me. When I came forward to tell, there was a big ruckus with a state investigation and a story in the paper. It made our school look bad so I was ostracized by the whole faculty, especially the principal. No one would even speak to me. It was as if I was the one who had done something wrong.

Amy, former fourth grade teacher

order to accomplish one's objectives and to get one's needs met. This violates the sense of benevolence required in a trusting relationship. The flight response also does damage to the long-term viability of the relationship: in avoiding the conflict, a person demonstrates a willingness to give up on the goals that fueled the relationship in the first place or to leave the relationship altogether.

In ongoing relationships such as those in schools, neither fight nor flight is likely to be productive as the predominant approach to conflict because both responses demonstrate a low commitment to the relationship. Other options exist. *Accommodation* is a conflict style that implies a stronger commitment to the relationship than to the task or goal and, therefore, a willingness to relinquish the goal. This reflects a "tend and befriend" response to conflict that is often seen among women or people with little power who are unable or unwilling to leave a relationship. Although acquiescing in any given situation may be an appropriate and acceptable response, a pattern of doing so over time will result in an imbalance in the relationship that sets the stage for eventual betrayal. *Compromise* is a balance between a commitment to the task and to the relationship and so implies a willingness to give up part of the goal in the interests of preserving the relationship.

Collaboration implies a strong commitment to both the relationship and the task, so that the parties negotiate a solution in which the needs of both parties are met. This can require creativity and a problem-solving focus because, by its very nature, conflict is about a seeming incompatibility of desires. But even passionately held differences can be negotiated when there is an underlying sense of trust and goodwill, a conviction that the other party will do what they can to avoid causing one harm. This takes not only a strong commitment, it also takes skills that many people, adults and children alike, have not mastered. In the next section, we'll see the toll that Fred's poor conflict-resolution skills and consequent conflict avoidance had on Fremont School.

The Keep-the-Peace Principal

Fred Martin was an affable, friendly man. His congenial manner-
isms and easy smile quickly put strangers and children at ease. Fred
liked pretty much everybody and wanted everybody to like him.
He liked to position himself near the front door each morning to
greet the teachers and students as they arrived at school. He especially made a point of greeting the more troubled and troublesome
students by name, encouraging them to make good choices and to
have a good day.

When Fred first become a principal, he enjoyed the status and
relatively low stress of the job. He expected primarily to be a manager, to make sure that the buses ran on time and that the building
was maintained in reasonable repair. With the pressures of the
accountability movement, however, everyone seemed to be looking
to the principal to make things right in schools. There were pressures from above and pressures from below and Fred felt squeezed in
the middle. Fred had always enjoyed his job, so he decided to just
do what he could do in the hours he was at school and not worry or
become stressed about the rest. Fred was not an instructional leader.
That had not been the expectation when he received his training,
and he readily admitted that he didn't have the skills to be one. He
fulfilled his obligation to visit classrooms twice a year and to complete a preprinted form. But having a conversation or giving sub-
stantive feedback tended to evoke an uncomfortable response, so
he generally gave everyone high ratings and left their evaluation
forms in their mailboxes to be signed and returned to him.

Although Fred talked the talk of high expectations, his lack of
follow-through when teachers violated even minimum standards,
and his leniency with students, led his faculty to discount his words.
His motivation seemed to be to avoid conflict at all costs. Fred lost
the trust of his faculty not through ill will, but through failure to
deal constructively with conflict. He lacked the courage and the
skills to deal with the inevitable conflicts inherent in running a

school, particularly one in an urban setting or one engaged in change.

Fred liked to think of himself as a progressive, collaborative leader. The faculty at Fremont appreciated Fred's openness with information and his willingness to include them in decisions that affected the functioning of the school. However, this inclusiveness allowed Fred to avoid some of the more unpleasant aspects of his job, like holding resistant faculty members accountable to the agreed-upon program of the school. The faculty saw Fred's use of shared decision making as an excuse for him to abdicate responsibility and avoid conflict. In the name of collaboration, Fred delegated away most important decisions about the school. Paul spoke for many teachers at Fremont as he expressed his frustration at Fred's inability to make key decisions: "It's very hard for him to make an executive decision. He'll say, 'What do you think?' or 'What do we want to do as a staff?' That's fine as far as shared decision making goes, but if it concerns a really important issue I think he needs to make the decision. There are a lot of decisions we would like to see him make that we don't really feel are staff decisions. They're administrative decisions."

A major problem concerning the effectiveness at Fremont was a segment of the faculty that was simply not doing its job. Fred's continual empty threats and inability to hold teachers accountable for standards of conduct had worn thin with the faculty. Paul vented his frustration at Fred's empty demands:

> What bothers staff members is that they will identify a
> problem, like test scores at a certain grade level, and he'll
> say, "I won't tolerate this. I'm going to deal with this."
> And nothing is ever done—just so no waves are created.
> Or if it is somebody who is abusing sick time, who has
> no sick time but just never comes—it's, "You know, it's
> only a matter of time and they'll be gone." But it still
> continues and nothing happens. We have people here

who have never bought into our program, and every year he says, "You may want to consider transferring," but every year nothing happens. He needs to call them privately and say, "I will do everything for you; but you are not buying into our program. You need to leave." But he won't do it. And I think the staff would fall on their hands and knees and bow to him if he would do that. You cannot just be the facilitator—you have to be the leader.

A failure to follow through with threats can be as damaging to trust as the breaking of a promise. Although the recipients of a broken threat may consider the lenient person to be more likable, they also rate them as lower in trust (Lindskold & Bennett, 1973). Credible threats can be an important strategy in repairing damaged trust. Brian, a novice teacher at Fremont, echoed Paul's concerns: "We have teachers who are late every single day. It's very flagrant with some staff members and he needs to put his foot down and say, 'We expect you to be here at 8:30 and I expect you to stay until 3:45. And that's the way it's going to be.' But he won't. He doesn't do that."

Brian was put in a difficult position when he attempted to fill the gap left by Fred's unwillingness to take action. He continued: "We have people coming in late. That's something that should be dealt with. And it's not; he's not enforcing his rules. I spoke up in one of our meetings, so then I was laughed at. They said, 'Oh, now we have to stay late because of you.'" Brian felt ostracized and belittled because of his attempts to get the faculty to live up to even minimum contract requirements.

Poorly performing teachers don't just hurt their students, they can have a negative impact on their fellow teachers as well. Having faculty members who neglect their duties, and do so with impunity, has a debilitating effect on a school, as Michael Fullan (2003) has noted: "Nothing undermines the motivation of hard-working teachers more than poor performance in other teachers being ignored over long periods of time. Not only do poor performing teachers negatively affect the students in their classes, but they also have a spillover effect by poisoning the overall climate of the school" (p. 78).

Brian was cognizant of the toll the lack of accountability was having on his own commitment level. He was disappointed to watch his own principles slipping. "The kids leave at 3:15. We're supposed to be here until 3:45. I'll find myself leaving at 3:30 sometimes because it's like, 'Why should I stay here? No one else is here.' So I find that my moral obligation is less because no one else is doing it. I can say I'm staying because that's the rule. I can have that moral fiber and I still think I do, but then I also think, 'What good is it going to do me to sit here for 15 more minutes when I could go do something else?'" Fred had a hard time motivating his faculty to stay late and work hard when he often left shortly after school ended himself.

Not only was Brian's commitment to his contract undermined by the general apathy in the school, the impact was also felt in his classroom. The low level of trust in the building and the lack of support were interfering with the developing sense of competence of this novice teacher. Brian reported:

> As a new teacher, that kind of lack of accountability, lack of guidance, it hurts. I'm not supported. I need to have an experienced teacher say, "Have you tried this?" I've learned to shoot from the hip, and that's sad. Some of the stuff has already been done and you don't realize it. You think you're doing something great and then someone says, "Oh, that's been done." You're, like, "Well thank you!" I want to make it real for the kids, and I'm still trying to learn to do that. I swear, if I didn't have to fight discipline all the time I don't know what kind

teacher I would be but I think I would be a fantastic one. I find myself to a point where—I was always hoping I wouldn't be a teacher that would raise my voice and yell at a child. But I have yelled and I feel sick.

The lack of support and accountability left Brian disappointed in the kind of teacher he was becoming. This young teacher had a genuine desire to have a positive impact on his students and to create engaging learning opportunities for them. Indeed, he might have been a fine teacher had he started his career in a setting that had offered more support and guidance, not to mention better role models. This young man, who began his career with a strong sense of commitment and caring for the low-income children he taught, might never fulfill his potential.

There were other ways that Fred's lack of leadership left his teachers feeling unsupported and unprotected. In the name of shared decision making, Fred had delegated all faculty complaints to a faculty council. Complaints were to be made in writing and the whole process was to be strictly confidential. When Kelli, a first grade teacher at Fremont, tried to use the council to address a concern about another teacher, however, the situation became very unpleasant. Kelli reported that often the teacher who was supposed to share recess duty with her simply did not show up. Kelli was put in the difficult position of having to supervise the entire playground by herself. This other teacher was also consistently late to pick up her students at the end of recess, so that Kelli and her class lost learning time waiting for the other class to be retrieved. When Kelli took this concern to the council, there was a breach in confidentiality and word of her complaint quickly spread. Instead of getting the help she requested, Kelli was subjected to a harsh tongue lashing by the other teacher and was ostracized by that teacher's friends. As a result of this incident, Kelli said she had given up on communicating about her problems to the principal or to the faculty council. She had decided that she would rather do her best to cope with the problem alone than to subject herself to a repeat performance of what she had endured.

Another of the ways that the faculty felt betrayed by Fred was in his taking credit for results that were almost wholly the result of teacher efforts. When Paul applied for and received a large grant for the school, he resented Fred's report to the school board in which he claimed credit for the grant. When the school began to show gains on test scores, teachers resented his boasting about how "we" raised scores, although he had provided very little in the way of instructional leadership. These boasts would not have seemed like such violations if Fred had played a more active role in assisting teachers to accomplish these goals.

Teachers at Fremont distrusted Fred because of his lack of reliability and competence. His integrity was also questioned when he failed to follow through on what he said he would do. Most of the faculty acknowledged that Fred meant well and they trusted in his benevolent intentions. But when they couldn't count on him to deal with serious problems at the school, hold teachers accountable to their obligation to students, and make difficult decisions, they were left feeling very vulnerable. His desire to keep peace and avoid conflict created disharmony and distrust. At Fremont School, without the leadership to cultivate and maintain productive working relationships, the environment was strained and difficult for all the participants.

For principals to engender trust, it takes more than just being nice. Avoiding holding people accountable for their responsibilities within the school may have helped Fred cultivate the perception of being a pleasant person, but it did not engender trust. Faculty were frustrated by Fred's failure to enforce even minimal rules, such as arrival and departure times of faculty, much less the abuse of sick time or aides who refused to do the work they were assigned. When Fred, in the name of shared decision making, tried to get teachers to police their own ranks but did not take action to back their attempts to deal with wayward teachers, the faculty felt betrayed.

A Debilitating Culture of Distrust

Although we sometimes have no choice but to rely on someone we distrust, those are situations we normally would prefer to avoid. Whether it is a person we once trusted who has betrayed us, or someone we never grew to trust in the first place, it is uncomfortable to find ourselves in a relationship of interdependence in which our objectives cannot be met without the involvement of that person. Distrust is not necessarily an irrational or unwise response in these situations but may be based on knowledge, experience, and a real difference in values (Barber, 1983). Distrust tends to provoke feelings of anxiety and insecurity, causing people to feel ill at ease and expend energy on monitoring the behavior and possible motives of others (Govier, 1992).

Distrust can be costly. As trust declines, the costs of doing business increase because people must engage in self-protective actions and continually make provisions for the possibility that another person will manipulate the situation for their own advantage (Limerick & Cunnington, 1993). When teachers or students feel unsafe, energy that could be devoted to teaching and learning is diverted to self-protection. In the absence of trust, people are increasingly unwilling to take risks and demand greater protections to defend their interests (Tyler & Kramer, 1996). People may use various means to protect themselves from the possible harm of the distrusted person and minimize their vulnerability. Subordinates may withhold information or use pretense or even deception to protect their interests. Administrators often resort to increased use of control mechanisms such as enforcing cumbersome rules and using excessive monitoring to protect themselves. Although such steps may be necessary and important, they typically are counterproductive (Govier, 1992).

One of the most difficult things about distrust is that once it is established it has a tendency to be self-perpetuating. When interacting with a distrusted person, even normally benign actions are regarded with suspicion. The negative beliefs about the other lead the suspicious person to discount any evidence that would help overcome distrust (Govier, 1992). The behavior of the distrusted person is systematically interpreted in such a way that distrust is confirmed. The very communication needed to restore trust is regarded with suspicion, so that suspicion builds on itself. Administrators whose words hold no credibility have lost the very tool they need to restore trust.

A lack of trust not only makes for an unpleasant or uncomfortable working environment, it also has a negative impact on the overall effectiveness of the organization. This was evident at Fremont, where student achievement scores were abysmally low. Betrayals can damage morale and the ability of workers to collaborate. Productivity and motivation also are likely to suffer. When broken promises by management were examined in one study, distrust was significantly related to deterioration in the employee's performance and to intentions to leave the employer (Robinson, 1996). When there was high initial trust between an employee and the manager, the employee's reactions to a perceived breach were much less severe; however, when the initial trust was low, the breach was much more likely to result in poor employee performance and the desire to leave the organization. The consequences of a cycle of distrust in a school include a deterioration of the quality and

---

WHEN I TOOK OVER as principal at the high school, I knew I would have my work cut out for me earning the trust of the faculty because there had been a great deal of hostility and animosity between the teachers and the previous administration. I made a point of positioning myself near the teachers' mailboxes in the morning to greet and get to know the teachers. I got a taste for just how tough the challenge was going to be one of the first mornings, when after I'd said, "Good morning! How are you?" to one of the teachers, I overheard her muttering to a colleague on the way out, "I wonder what she means by that!"

Pat, high school principal

effectiveness of communication and shared decision making, as well as a decline in the citizenship and commitment of the teachers.

Constrained Communication

Schools need open communication to be effective, and distrust is likely to have a deleterious effect on communication patterns. When one is interacting with a distrusted person, especially if that person holds more power within an organizational hierarchy, the goal of communication often becomes the protection of one's interest and the reduction of one's anxiety rather than the accurate transmission of ideas. A person may feel compelled to be evasive or to distort attitudes or information when communicating with a distrusted person. In an organizational culture of distrust, subordinates acknowledge a great tendency to withhold information and distort upward communication (Roberts & O'Reilly, 1974).

Teachers in low-trust schools describe constrained communication networks. In a climate of suspicion, teachers are guarded as to who they talk to and what they say. As we saw in Kelli's disastrous run-in with the faculty council at Fremont, although teachers acknowledged that there were significant problems in their schools, they were unwilling to reveal such problems and work to resolve them for fear of retaliation. Communication is often blocked or distorted to avoid confrontation. The communication between principals and teachers is hampered by distrust. Where trust is low, teachers may avoid making contact with the principal, thereby making it difficult for him or her to gain the information needed to be proactive. When there is a high level of trust between principals and teachers, teachers are more likely to have higher levels of confidence in the accuracy of information coming from the principal, greater satisfaction with communication, and a greater desire for interaction with the principal (Roberts & O'Reilly, 1974). We saw such a pattern of productive communication between Brenda and the Brookside teachers. Open communication that flows from the

OUR PRINCIPAL NEVER has the courage to confront a concern directly with a teacher. He always couches it saying he has had calls "from concerned parents." One time the whole school was gathered on the bleachers for an assembly when we learned that the presenter had not arrived. The kids were getting restless, so as one teacher ran to the office to make phone calls and see what was going on, another grabbed her guitar and two of her friends started to dance, putting on a silly, impromptu performance. The principal must have seen them from his office window because later he called in those teachers to say that he had had "some calls from parents" who thought their performance was unprofessional. But that was a lie because where they were wasn't visible from the street!

Pam, second grade teacher

people "in the trenches" can be a tremendous asset to a principal in orchestrating school improvement.

Confined Decision Making

There are two motivations for involving teachers in decisions concerning the life of the school. The first motivation is simply to increase teachers' satisfaction, loyalty, and acceptance of decisions. There is recognition that teachers have sufficient autonomy in schools that if they do not "buy in" to a decision, they can undermine the effectiveness of an initiative simply by withholding their full effort or even by actively sabotaging its implementation. In this model, which could be called "contrived collaboration," shared decision making is more form than substance; teachers' input is rarely taken seriously. Often the decision has already been made before teachers are asked to participate. In the second model, principals and teachers make decisions jointly. This model highlights teachers' competence and acknowledges that they have valuable knowledge and insights to bring to decisions. Higher quality decisions are the goal of this more genuine form of shared decision making that gives teachers actual influence over the outcomes of decisions that affect them (Pounder, 1998; Short & Greer, 1997).

Shared decision making, as it has typically been exercised in schools, has been criticized as most often being of the first model, affording teachers little real influence over organizational decisions that matter to them (Malen, Ogawa, & Kranz, 1990). This model is rooted in distrust, distrust both of teachers' potential contributions to decisions and their willingness to implement decisions faithfully. The second model requires a good deal more trust in teachers and their capability to act in the best interests of the school community rather than narrow self-interest (Hoy & Tarter, 2003). When principals "talk the talk" of shared decision making but simply go through the motions, as in the first model, trust is undermined by raising teachers' expectations and creating cynicism when words don't match actions.

When principals extend trust to teachers through shared control, they provoke greater trust from teachers. The level of shared decision making in a school is significantly related to the level of faculty trust in the principal (Tschannen-Moran, 2001). Paradoxically, when teachers have greater trust in the principal, this trust may actually decrease the need for teachers to be involved in as many decisions. When teachers feel confident that their interests will be well looked after, they may be more willing to extend decision-making authority to the principal and abide by the decisions that are made (Tyler & Degoey, 1996).

In general, teachers appreciate being asked to participate in decisions about issues that affect them, as they did at Fremont. This pleasure is likely to sour, however, when they perceive that their involvement has no real impact, that they are blamed when the decisions do not work out the way they had hoped, or that the principal is simply using faculty participation to abdicate responsibility for accountability within the school.

Corroded Citizenship and Commitment

Organizational citizenship has to do with instances when a worker spontaneously goes beyond the formally prescribed job requirements and performs nonmandatory behaviors without expectation of receiving explicit recognition or compensation (Organ, 1988; Deluga, 1994). Organ (1997) emphasized the importance of organizational citizenship in promoting organizational effectiveness, noting that "organizational citizenship behaviors are vital for productivity because organizations cannot forecast through stated job descriptions the entire spectrum of subordinate behaviors needed for achieving goals" (p. 4). These kinds of behaviors are particularly important for schools, where formal job descriptions can, at best, delineate broad parameters for the expectations of teachers' responsibilities. When citizenship behaviors such as courtesy, conscientiousness, sportsmanship, and civic virtue are absent, organizational life is likely to be strained. These strains were evident in the frustrations expressed by the teachers at Fremont. If schools attempt to require citizenship activities, however, they may engender resistance and resentment.

Transformational leadership behaviors are leadership behaviors that are considered to spur employees to go beyond minimum requirements and give their best for the organization. Transformational leadership describes the behavior of a leader who has articulated a clear vision, is able to foster an acceptance of group goals, and holds high performance expectations while providing an appropriate model for followers to emulate. A transformational leader provides individualized support and intellectual stimulation. Transformational leadership behaviors have been found to lead to greater citizenship behavior of subordinates but *only* if the employees trust the leader. When employees did not trust the leader, these leadership behaviors did not lead to greater citizenship (Podsakoff, MacKenzie, Moorman, & Fetter, 1990; Tschannen-Moran, 2003). The implications for schools are significant. For school leaders to be effective, they must earn the trust of the people who work for them.

At Fremont, organizational citizenship was very low. It's not just that the teachers put forth the minimum required by their contract, they put in the minimum they could get away with. Teachers reported that many of their colleagues came late and left early and abused the sick leave allotted in their contract. Teachers reported teaching assistants who spent their time in the office chatting with the secretaries, even during the ninety-minute block of intensive instructional time in the mornings when they were most needed in the classrooms, or who refused to do recess duty even if they were assigned to do it. Kelli reported that an aide had even eaten the snacks that had been prepared for students to eat during their break from standardized testing! At Lincoln, Allisha reported a veteran teacher who watched soap operas every afternoon while his class was assigned seat work. Because this man was outwardly compliant and often acted as the principal designee when Gloria was out of the building, she turned a blind eye to this behavior but harassed the much more dedicated teachers who questioned her.

Teachers at both Fremont and Lincoln struggled to maintain their own dedication and commitment in an atmosphere that did not support that effort. For some, poor citizenship led to disillusionment with the whole enterprise of teaching. Allisha, a second year teacher at Lincoln, questioned whether she would remain in the teaching profession: "That's why I'm in school now, because I can't see retiring as a teacher. I thought that we would have much more respect as teachers. I was expecting more respect from our principal and basically we get no respect. She gives more respect to the assistants that work in this building. She gives them something to do and they won't do it. But let us say that, it's a whole different story, you know."

The teachers interviewed at Fremont and Lincoln had either put in for transfers or felt they needed to give a rationalization for staying. They spoke of caring about the children and wanting to make things better for their low-income students. Rob described how many of his hours outside of school were spent attending his students' sporting events and concerts. He described lying awake at night thinking about his students and how he could address the difficulties they were having. During the winter months, Rob purchased many sets of hats and mittens for his students. Even students who were not in his class would come to him for these things when word got around. As much as these teachers cared about their students and the work they were doing, in the absence of a concerted effort by the entire faculty, there was a general sense of discouragement.

Where trust was high, the level of organizational citizenship also tended to be high (Jones & George, 1998; Tschannen-Moran, 2003). At Brookside, teachers were not only considerate of one another, they went far beyond the minimum required of them. Kathy described the faculty's reaction to Brenda's expectation that every teacher make at least one positive contact with every parent in his or her class within the first two weeks of school. "We could say no. Contractually we could say no. It's a pain, it takes time and work, and most of it you do from your home or you spend hours here at school. She expects it. She can't force us to do it because it's not contractual. Yet we have such a high respect for her, and we want her backing when something goes wrong, so we do it. I mean, we fuss and groan and grumble about things, but most of the time if she says, 'Do this,' then we try to do our best."

Each of the teachers interviewed at Brookside described ways that they willingly responded to requests to go beyond the minimum, from an annual Saturday planning retreat in the spring to a fall sleepover or other extra programs at the school. Brenda had earned the trust of her faculty by being a valuable resource in times of trouble. Whether teachers were struggling

A TEACHER IN our school made a mistake and cursed when she was yelling at a kid. The parents made a big issue out of it, and our principal just buckled under the pressure. She pressured the teacher into taking a leave of absence for the rest of the school year—six weeks before the end of the year. I doubt she'll be back next year. She is a really good teacher; she just lost her temper with this kid. Morale is really low. The whole faculty feels unprotected— like if a parent complained our principal would not back us up.

Caitlyn, middle school Spanish teacher

with the behavior of a particular student, how to plan and present a particular curricular unit, or how to cope with a difficult parent, the teachers reported that they could rely on her for help. In exchange, they were willing to work hard and give their best.

Putting It into Action

To be a trustworthy school leader takes courage. It also takes sensitivity. It takes a willingness to deal with difficult situations and difficult people in a straightforward and firm manner. A caring stance does not mean that teachers are not held accountable. On the contrary, your caring and commitment to students demand that you hold high expectations for teachers' performance. These high expectations are bolstered by the support and guidance to help teachers meet these standards. You need to blend pressing for goal achievement with demonstrating concern for teachers and staff. It takes wisdom and sensitivity to discern how to balance a task orientation with a focus on nurturing relationships, as one or the other may predominate in particular circumstances and situations. But overall your leadership of the school will need to evidence both support and challenge in good measure.

Key Points About Betrayal

- The initial reaction to betrayal is often stunned disbelief that later turns to anger and the desire for revenge.

- Betrayal occurs when dissatisfaction with the current situation causes a drop in the benevolence, integrity, and openness of the trusted person.

- Violations of trust in schools tend to stem from a damaged sense of civic order or from damage to a person's or a group's sense of identity.

- Avoidance of conflict is an act of moral neglect that is likely to lead to distrust of the leader.

- When forced to work with a distrusted person, people are likely to feel ill at ease. This discomfort may motivate them to protect themselves by withholding or even distorting information.

- In a climate of distrust, teachers are unlikely to give their best efforts to the school and its mission. In such a climate, shared decision making is often a sham.

Questions for Reflection and Discussion

1. When have you felt betrayed at work and what was your reaction? Did the violation stem from a damaged sense of civic order or from a damaged identity? How did you interpret the motivation of the perpetrator? Was trust ever restored? How?

2. To what extent does the culture in your school discourage betrayal through norms of openness, trust, and respect? Or is the culture of your school characterized by conflict over goals, negative internal politics, and shifting coalitions that lend themselves to betrayal?

3. How is conflict handled in your school? Is it avoided and suppressed or does it tend to get ugly and out of control? Or is conflict handled constructively? What are the consequences of this conflict style? How could the quality of dialogue be improved with training in better conflict management skills?

4. If avoiding conflict causes distrust, do you think you should go out of your way to bring hidden conflicts within your school to the surface?

5. What instances have you witnessed in which a sense of betrayal has lowered people's commitment, interfered with their performance, and increased their desire to leave the school?

5

Revenge

Revenge is best served cold.

Spanish proverb

When we have trusted someone, we have held certain expectations of that person in a situation in which we felt vulnerable. If those expectations were not met, and our trust has been betrayed, we must decide how to respond. Whether the response leads to the restoration of trust or an escalation of conflict depends on the choices made by the actors in the situation. Trust ebbs and flows as parties choose how to respond to instances of broken trust, either by engaging in the effort required to repair the relationship or by choosing various forms of revenge.

When a violation of trust has occurred, the way the victim understands the cause of the violation affects the likely response, and specifically whether there is a desire for revenge. Among people recounting on-the-job experiences of betrayal, when the victim concluded that an action was outside the control of the perpetrator, revenge was not sought; however, when the victim held the perpetrator responsible for the violation, there was motivation to seek revenge (Bies & Tripp, 1996). Blame was assigned and revenge sought when the victim perceived the behavior to have grown out of selfishness or malevolence on the part of the perpetrator. Victims also assigned responsibility to the system or organization as a whole for hiring or failing to constrain the perpetrator.

There are a number of revenge strategies victims may consider. Some people enjoy indulging in revenge fantasies, conjuring up elaborate pictures of how the perpetrator might be hurt or publicly humiliated. Although they don't intend to act on these fantasies, there is comfort in imagining that "justice will be done." Other victims express their anger and outrage in public ways, recounting the betrayal to others to stir up sympathy and harm the reputation of the perpetrator. The victim's act of revenge may then provoke a sense of betrayal on the part of the perpetrator. This can spark a self-perpetuating cycle of feuding, each side engaging in a tit-for-tat volley of insults, snubs, and betrayal, thereby fueling a spiral of distrust.

Some victims simply withdraw from any social contact with the person who has betrayed them. Others seek to restore the relationship by arranging for a private confrontation to make the perpetrator aware of their hurt, anger, and disappointment in order to negotiate a resolution. For example, if the victim felt that she had suffered a damaged sense of identity, she might seek the restoration of her reputation. Based on an apology, an acknowledgment, or a commitment to behave differently in the future, victims might be willing to offer forgiveness. There is power in forgiveness because the victim, not the perpetrator, restores trust. Some harms, however, may be irreversible—in these circumstances the victim may be unwilling ever again to extend trust to the person who has caused him or her harm (Bies & Tripp, 1996).

Revenge is not solely an emotional reaction to violation; a good deal of thinking and planning go on as well. A victim's initial reaction to learning of a betrayal is often feelings of disorientation and stunned disbelief. This confusion

---

OUR PRINCIPAL ACCUSED some teachers of entering his computer after hours to look at his evaluation records. A few days later, he parked in a handicapped parking space and one of the teachers alerted the police, who ticketed him.

Tanya, middle school teacher

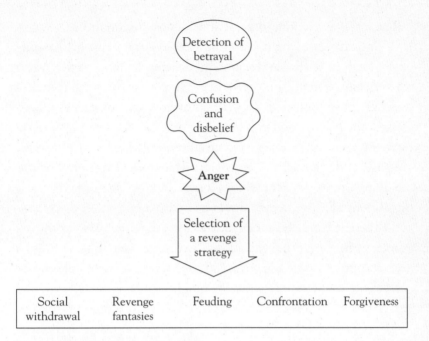

Figure 5.1. The Path of Revenge

usually turns to anger as the reality of what had occurred sets it. Contrary to stereotypic notions, however, a study of revenge revealed victims' choice of revenge strategy to be "cool and calculated, . . . it appeared to be quite rational in both deliberation and delivery" (Bies & Tripp, 1996, p. 259). A complicating factor in the dynamics of revenge, however, is evidence of "different arithmetics" between victim and perpetrator, whereby each assesses the cost of the perceived damage differently. These different calculations, and the responses they evoke, play a role in the escalation process of a conflict. Upon reflection, people are likely to "discover" more malevolence on the part of the perpetrators, thus enhancing blame, paranoid cognitions, and conspiracy theories that may lead victims to seek social support and reinforcement for their perceptions.

Betrayal may lead not only to a motivation for revenge, it can also lead to resentment. Solomon and Flores draw a distinction between revenge and resentment:

"Revenge is quick, indeed, sometimes almost instantaneous. (When it is immediate, it might better be viewed as retaliation.) Resentment tends to be slow and simmering, steeped far more in the dream of vengeance than in its actuality. That is precisely what makes resentment so dangerous, for whereas revenge can sometimes indeed restore the balance and provide a level playing field on which to restart negotiation and renew mutual understanding, resentment, because of its clandestine and defensive nature, does not allow for that opportunity" (Solomon & Flores, 2001, pp. 142–143).

Resentment is directed not at a situation but rather directly at other people (one's boss, one's colleagues, the executives of the organization). Resentment leads to distrust because it also tends to be vengeful. A resentful person "allows his own sense of importance and wounded merit to fester inside him until he is poisoned by it and incapable of creative or constructive action" (Solomon & Flores, 2001, p. 112). A school culture that embodies a mood of resentment can lead to deterioration of performance, low initiative, and diminished trust among coworkers. Sabotage and other forms of collective action in organizations in defiance of the interests of the institution or its management are typically a product of resentment.

Revenge is not always altogether negative, however. It can also play a potentially positive role in organizational life (Bies & Tripp, 1996). Not only can revenge act as a constraint against abuse of power and injustice, it can also promote cooperation and be a potent motivator for constructive change. In an act of revenge after a year of being subjected to insults and blame on the part of their new principal, the teachers of one urban elementary school all refused to sign their contracts until they received assurances that the principal would not return the following year. Teachers in an upscale suburban community got

MY MOTTO IS, "Don't get mad, get even." My principal laid into me in a faculty meeting in front of my colleagues. I'm going to make him sorry. The next time he wants anything from me, anything at all, the answer is just going to be, "No."

Jeff, high school history teacher

revenge for the demeaning remarks about teachers made by the superintendent during a difficult contract negotiation session by initiating a petition drive to pressure the superintendent to retract the statements. With the assistance of the PTA, the teachers printed the petition with hundreds of signatures in a full-page advertisement in the local newspaper. The superintendent publicly apologized for making the remarks. Revenge has a way of equalizing some of the power differential in organizations. It gives victims a choice of how to respond to a breach in trust, and it gives them some control as to if and when they will again offer their trust. The next section details how the faculty at Lincoln felt betrayed by Gloria and of the tactics they used to seek revenge.

The Overzealous Reformer

Gloria Davies saw herself as a reformer with the best interests of the children at heart. When she took over the principalship, she was determined to make immediate changes in how things were done at Lincoln School and to get rid of any teachers who didn't want to come along. By pressing ahead before building trust with her faculty, however, Gloria alienated people and became engaged in a power struggle with her teachers. At a faculty meeting during her first year at the school, Gloria assailed the teachers for their lack of success with student test scores. When the teachers protested about the many challenges they faced in educating low-income students, Gloria responded in a matter-of-fact tone, "OK, I want you to bring me a list of the names of all of the students in your classes that you don't think you can bring up to standard." She continued, "Then we're going to bring them all to the auditorium and take their pictures. We're going to hold a press conference because the parents and the community have a right to know which of their children we can't educate." This confrontational and condemning stance made it clear that Gloria was not a resource they could count on to assist with the many challenges they faced.

Instead of taking the time to invest in relationship building before embarking on a systematic change process in which she involved the teachers who were close to the action of the school, who understood the culture of the community and the school, and who would ultimately have to implement any changes, she forged ahead in a top-down, "my way or the highway" approach. Gloria took too much responsibility for change at Lincoln and failed to recognize that principals get much of their work done through other people. It is the teachers who do the central work of school, and it is the job of administrators to create the context for teaching and learning. When the teachers resisted Gloria's initiatives, she asserted her authority, thus setting the stage for the ensuing power struggle.

By the third year of her tenure at Lincoln, the power struggle had become intense, morale had plummeted, and even teachers who had been initially willing to give her the benefit of the doubt and work with Gloria began to lose faith. Teachers referred to the school as a war zone. There was an atmosphere of fear at the school and teachers were guarded in what they said for fear of reprisals. Student achievement had failed to make the kinds of gains Gloria had hoped for when she took leadership of the school.

In various ways Gloria fell short across all the facets of trust—good will, integrity, openness, reliability, and competence. Gloria's failure to establish trust was particularly due to a perceived lack of good will or benevolence toward the teachers. Teachers' complaints centered on Gloria's failure to provide them with adequate support. Teachers also saw her tactics as manipulative and dishonest. For example, Gloria lost the faith of her faculty because of the means she employed to remove a struggling young teacher. Gloria initially challenged this teacher about her use of sick days on Fridays and Mondays. The teacher countered that she had used these days to take her young daughter to the doctor and that she was within the number of sick days allowed for in her contract. When the teacher contacted Rob, the union representative in the building, and asked him to be a part of any subsequent meetings on the subject, Gloria responded by questioning the teacher's competence. Gloria initiated an aggressive schedule of observation and evaluation of the teacher. Other teachers were angered by what they saw as the unfair treatment of this young teacher and worried that they could become victims of the same treatment if they were to challenge the principal. Allisha, a second year teacher at Lincoln recounted the incident:

> We just felt like after the first observation and evaluation that our principal was on a mission to get rid of her, and nothing she could have done would stop it. She even asked to be placed back in the Peer Assistance and Review program and she was turned down for that. So there was nothing she could do. When Gloria was telling her that she didn't have control of her classroom, she was asking, "Well, what can I do? You are supposed to be giving me support. Give me advice, what can I do?" But none was offered. So we knew right then and there that she wanted her out. Gloria has always been nice to me, but then she was to the other teacher also. So you never know when she'll turn on you.

Although other teachers acknowledged that this teacher was having difficulty with classroom management, they faulted Gloria with not offering guidance and assistance before orchestrating her removal.

Trust in Gloria was further damaged when she tried to remove several teachers who were informal leaders, well-liked and respected by the rest of the faculty, in order to bring in staff members she knew who would be more compliant to her wishes. Because other teachers identified with the victims, distrust spread among the faculty. One of these was Rob Stevens, a popular and well-respected fifth grade teacher who had taught at Lincoln for a decade. In his capacity as union representative, Rob had come into conflict with Gloria, filing numerous grievances on behalf of various teachers in the school. At the beginning of the school year, Gloria announced at a faculty meeting, without prior consultation with Rob, that he was being assigned to teach second grade. Allisha described how the tactic was seen by the faculty as blatantly manipulative and as a means to get him to transfer out of the building:

> At the beginning of the year we had a staff reduction. We had an opening in second grade and we had an opening in a four-five split. So we had a staff meeting and she came in and told us about the staff reduction. Then the next thing we know she goes, "Mrs. Johnson, you'll be teaching the four-five split, and Mr. Stevens (who had been teaching fifth grade for ten years!), you will be teaching second grade. Thank you. That's the end of our meeting. Goodbye." She turned around and walked away. Everyone turned and looked at Rob and asked, "When did she tell you this?" He said, "This is the first I've heard it." She hadn't discussed it with him; she just announced it and that was that. We just knew instantly that he was going to transfer out. Everyone felt that that's what she wanted. But he didn't. He said he wasn't going to let her pull that one over on him. But he just feels betrayed because of what she did.

The betrayal was motivated by a negative assessment of the current situation such that there was little concern for the impact this move might have on Rob. This was followed by a drop in Gloria's integrity as she constructed a rationale based on a set of principles not shared by Rob and other members of the faculty about an appropriate process for classroom reassignment.

Another incident involved Mary, a teacher who had initially worked very closely with Gloria to see her vision of turning the school around realized. Mary had worked to get a number of grants and special programs for the school. When Mary finally got fed up because of the lack of cooperation and appreciation, she started refusing special assignments. Gloria responded by trying to remove Mary from her position, a move that left Mary feeling hurt and betrayed. Mary felt doubly betrayed when Gloria's means of doing so was by calling into question her competence.

> I keep on getting things thrown in my mailbox. It is addressed to the principal and it will be thrown in my box—about grants to write or a committee to chair. Now I just throw it back. So I finally wrote a note back and said, "I do not want to chair this committee, but I will be happy to participate." And that was read at a staff meeting, that that's what I had said, verbatim. Verbatim! . . . I had said to certain staff members that it would either be on the bulletin or she would find a way to let the whole staff know that I declined. After that, she told me I wasn't strong enough in my position and that she wanted someone else.

Although Mary felt deeply betrayed by Gloria, she nonetheless recognized that Gloria's negative behavior was caused, at least in part, by frustration after three years of trying to get the teachers to try new things or do more than the minimum required of them. She acknowledged that Gloria had come to the school with ideas for improving the curriculum but was discouraged by the lack of progress that had been made: "I can understand her frustration, and I can deal with that. I have seen people show an interest and then turn around and not put in any effort on the follow through. But I can't take responsibility for all the people on the staff and their unwillingness to learn." Although Mary acknowledged that Gloria was both tired and frustrated, and with good reason, she was nonetheless disappointed by the lack of leadership and the consequences this had for both teachers and students.

Teachers wanted reassurance that their principal would be fair and accurate in their evaluations and would not use these manipulatively. They also wanted to be sure that fair procedures were followed, whether in classroom and duty assignments or in the hiring of new staff. Integrity is demonstrated by a convergence of actions and words. Integrity was compromised when one person was told one thing and someone else was given a different answer to the same question. At Lincoln, there was resentment that Gloria had given negative assessments of teaching performance to teachers she wanted to replace with teachers of her own choosing, even though she had previously been complimentary of these same teachers. The pretense of an open hiring process to fill openings was also suspect when there were indications that she already had in mind the replacements she wanted to hire.

The effects of broken trust were multiplied when the teachers turned to each other for support, recounting the details of an infraction or an incident in which a teacher did not receive support, so that trust was also broken with all who listened empathetically and worried that they might be a victim of the same kind of treatment. The gossip served to broaden the negative impact of these incidents beyond the teachers involved and drive down trust among the whole faculty.

One incident, reported by Rob, entailed a violation of both civic order and a sense of identity. The situation involved a group of teachers, of which Rob was a part, who had served on a committee to put together a technology plan for the school to take advantage of a statewide program for schools. Although none of the teachers had any experience or training in grant writing or in technology, they had worked hard to do the necessary research, giving up time after school and during their spring break to write the proposal. Gloria was a member of the committee, but she rarely came to meetings or offered any assistance. Despite all their efforts, the proposal was not funded. When Rob arrived early to a faculty meeting, he overheard Gloria talking to a district official about the plan's rejection. Gloria's harsh remarks about the incompetence of the committee left Rob feeling hurt and unappreciated. He felt especially betrayed because Gloria had not carried her weight as a member of the committee. There was the sense that had the proposal been funded, Gloria would gladly have accepted credit for the process, but when it was rejected she blamed the committee members and failed to acknowledge her lack of leadership. Rob expressed reluctance to volunteer for any future committees.

Openness is another dimension of trust where Gloria fell short. Studies of trust in organizations across hierarchical lines have proposed that openness would be important for subordinates to develop trust in their superiors because withholding important information is one way that superiors maintain power or manipulate employees (Kramer, 1996; Mishra, 1996). At Lincoln School, Gloria's lack of engagement with the rest of the faculty was a source of distrust. Rob described the situation this way: "I see the worker bees and the Queen. The Queen stays in her hive, or in her office in this case. Everyone else is on the front line out here; we are working and getting the job done to the best of our ability. It is almost like two different worlds. And the only time they cross is maybe a discipline issue. It's almost like an island down there. We're out here working, you know, fighting the war and there's no support."

Gloria was described as inaccessible, and when interactions did occur the tone was often negative and unhelpful. Rob continued: "There is becoming a distinction between the workers and the managers. It is almost like the Wizard of Oz behind the drape, and you can't see, you can't talk to the Wizard. You know they're there but you can't communicate with them."

Teachers at Lincoln were very guarded in their own communication as well. When asked about incidents of broken trust at Lincoln, Allisha began, "I'll be vague about it." Mary switched the public address system to a privacy setting in the room where she was being interviewed. She was visibly shaken when a message came through over the system from the office, and it took several moments for her to regain her composure sufficiently to continue. She was reassured somewhat when she realized that the privacy setting might mean that information from the office could be transmitted to the room without the reverse being true. She nonetheless seemed to be mentally rehearsing what had just been said to see whether she had said anything incriminating or had disclosed anything for which she might be punished. At the conclusion of the interview, Mary looked around furtively in the hallway and stairwell to be sure they were empty and led me out a back entrance in order that we not be seen. Each of the Lincoln teachers interviewed wanted reassurance that their confidentiality would be protected.

At Lincoln School, a pervasive cycle of distrust had set in, making the faculty suspicious of the principal's motives for almost any action. Teachers reported breaches of civic order or what they felt was owed to them and to their colleagues, as well as assaults on their identities as professionals and as people. The incidents had an impact both on the teachers' performance and their desire to remain a part of the organization. Although these teachers still felt a commitment to the children of their school and wanted to work hard based on their own sense of professionalism, they reported less than full effort by many of their peers. Of the three teachers interviewed, Rob and Mary had put in requests to transfer to other schools, and Allisha, a second-year teacher, expressed doubts about how long she would remain in the teaching profession. The consequences to the organization of the loss of trust were substantial.

A Culture of Control

One of the most difficult aspects of distrust in an organization is that it can lead to a culture of control. The classic authoritarian bureaucracy is based on the foundational assumption that teachers, like workers in general, are untrustworthy. The hierarchy has as its basic goal the control and monitoring of teachers. The role of the system is to ensure that potentially reluctant and irresponsible teachers do what is prescribed by the school organization. The behavior of the leader serves to reinforce the distrust embedded in the system. Decisions are concentrated at the top in the hands of a few and flow down the chain of command. Directives from superiors are to be followed without question and regardless of the situation. Taken to the extreme, the culture of control leads to micromanagement, rigidity, and a proliferation of dysfunctional rules.

Micromanagement

One common way that distrust is evident in leadership practice is in the micromanagement of workers. Micromanaging is a failure of trust. It is a triumph of perfectionism and ego. Closely supervising subordinates, overspecifying job requirements by telling capable people how to do their job, or redoing work that has been done by a subordinate to meet perfectionist standards shows disrespect and a lack of trust in the individual. Subordinates sense this and are likely to become resentful and withdrawn, withholding both ideas and effort. This withholding has a detrimental effect on schools, where excellence can only be reached when all organizational participants give their very best.

Rigidity

It is not uncommon for organizations to respond to a perceived external threat by becoming more rigid and controlling, thus hindering the effective operation of the organization or its ability to adapt in response to the threat (Mintzberg, 1989). Schools are currently experiencing just such a perceived threat to their legitimacy. But becoming more rigid is often precisely the wrong direction to go. Quite often, such situations require that the organization become more flexible, innovative, and adaptive. Trust is an enormous resource to organizations experiencing crisis

OUR SUPERINTENDENT IS a control freak. It is a small district, so he thinks he can keep his fingers in everything. He'll show up at the school unannounced and you'll come across him squatting outside a classroom listening to what's going on inside. When the weather is good, you'll find him lurking around outside under the open classroom windows, listening.

Todd, assistant principal

because it helps them avoid rigidity and a "hunkering down" mentality (Mishra, 1996). Communication flows more easily and resources are shared rather than hoarded so that they can be allocated in ways that will have the greatest benefit for the survival of the organization.

A Proliferation of Rules

Rules are a necessary part of organizational life. Like all organizations, schools must find ways to balance extending trust to employees at various levels of the organization with the creation of safeguards against self-serving or dishonest behavior. Schools adopt rules, procedures, and other formal organizational mechanisms to guide behavior. However, formal controls instituted to increase performance reliability can interfere with the achievement of the very goals they were put in place to serve. When trust breaks down, organizations are faced with deciding how to respond. As trust deteriorates in an organization, one likely response is the institution of rules to serve as a substitute for trust (Shapiro, 1987; Sitkin & Stickel, 1996; Zucker, 1986). Taken to the extreme, however, the proliferation of rules is likely to interfere with organizational effectiveness.

MY PRINCIPAL'S BIG thing is that lesson plans have to be done in a certain format—these little books. But I do big units with big ideas—I couldn't fit them all in those little boxes. If you said that you were reading pages 127–135 in the history book one week and your plans the next week didn't start on page 136, she'd call you in and ask you what happened. If your plans said that at 10:10 on Tuesday you were going to be doing phonics, if she came in at 10:10 you'd better be doing phonics or she would cream you. She threatened to write me up and send it over to central office. But just when she was about to do that, the letter arrived announcing that I had been named statewide teacher of the year— so she dropped it.

Nancy, fifth grade teacher

Standardized controls and rigid procedures can lead to a breakdown in efficiency and effectiveness in situations in which a certain amount of discretion is needed for workers to do their jobs effectively (Fox, 1974; Sitkin & Stickel, 1996). Rigid rules and regulations are likely to be effective only when the requirements of a task are understood well enough to be specified clearly and concisely. The work of schools is complex and changes as the needs of students vary. For teachers to work as professionals, they need the discretion to be responsive to the ever-changing demands of their students and curriculums.

It was noted earlier that schools are both bureaucratic and professional organizations. When schools are pervaded by a culture of control, they overemphasize the bureaucratic nature of the organization at the expense of the professional. Power is concentrated in the office of the administrator, and teachers are deprived of necessary professional discretion. In such schools, principals use their power and authority to control and discipline teachers and obstruct innovation. In enforcing a control mentality, the administration gets in the way rather than helping its teachers solve problems and do their work. Coercive rules and procedures punish subordinates rather than reward productive practices. Instead of promoting organizational learning, coercive procedures demand blind obedience and force reluctant subordinates to comply.

Coercive bureaucratic rules can undermine trust because they are based on the premise that workers desire to evade responsibilities and withhold proper and full performance of obligations. Extreme elaboration of bureaucratic rules and a lack of flexibility in the application of rules are likely to engender resistance and resentment because such rules communicate distrust to those to whom they are directed. The system is designed to monitor and control teachers and to enforce compliance to organizational directives (Adler & Borys, 1996).

At Lincoln School, Gloria turned to the imposition of rules to reassert her authority in an attempt to bring her faculty into compliance with her desires for the school. Rob described how over the course of a school year, when trust took a decided decline, rules came to take on increasing importance: "I was on the Building Council. The staff and principal get together and talk about issues in the school. At the beginning of the year, we would sit around and discuss and come up with options, whereas by the end of the year, Gloria would come with the teachers' contract book and would say, 'Well, it says this thing here and that is how we are going to handle it,' even when other options existed or were desirable. It has just been going by the book, and a very strict interpretation."

Rob resented going through the motions of a shared decision process when the real agenda seemed to be a game of using rules for Gloria to manipulate the staff. He also resented the arbitrariness with which Gloria exercised her formal authority in order to assert her power within the school. The imposition of rules in a capricious manner felt like an assault on the teachers' professionalism. Gloria's tactics to improve what she may have regarded as a lazy or unmotivated staff seemed destined for failure. Allisha complained: "There have been many edicts from up above, from the principal. At the beginning of the year, we were told we are no longer allowed to eat lunches in the library unless we have permission. We are professionals. There were no reasons, no input. And just numerous things like that throughout the year. Staff has been really unhappy. A lot of them just seem petty or trivial. If we could just have input, we might be more accepting of them. But that's never an option."

The teachers resented Gloria's tactics and saw them as an infringement of their professional status. They became less rather than more willing to cooperate with Gloria on her agenda. Although teachers reported that most people complied with the rules, many used their creativity to find ways to sabotage and thwart Gloria's efforts. The resulting power struggle did not bode well for the development of a professional school culture or improvement in the quality of the school's effectiveness for students.

Rigid and coercive rules negatively influence employees' affiliation with the school and can have detrimental effects on satisfaction and morale. More often than not, these procedures generate alienation, resentment, and hostility (Hoy, Blazovsky, & Newland, 1983). These are precisely the results we saw at Lincoln. Gloria's attempts to improve the performance outcomes at Lincoln by instituting standardized, one-size-fits-all procedures backfired because they stripped teachers of the discretion necessary to be responsive to student needs. Teachers and students alike may respond to a proliferation of rules with feelings of alienation, disloyalty, and lack of commitment, which ironically can make dishonesty and cheating more prevalent (Govier, 1992; Walker, 1999). A cycle of distrust can ensue as more rules are put into place in response to increasing instances of broken trust.

Rules That Facilitate

The system of written rules, policies, and procedures in schools need not be coercive; they can also be facilitating. Policies and procedures can be flexible guides to help solve problems rather than constraints that create them. As guidelines, they reflect "best practices" and help subordinates deal with surprises and crises and assist employees with solutions to problems in their work (Adler & Borys, 1996). Organizational participants are encouraged to reflect on innovative ways to respond to novel situations and not adhere blindly to rules and regulations. Flexibility and professional judgment temper or even substitute for rigid rules and procedures. Enabling procedures invite interactive dialogue; they require participation and collaboration. Facilitative strategies allow problems to be viewed as opportunities, differences to be valued, and mistakes to be capitalized on and learned from (Hoy & Sweetland, 2001). Improvement is the objective.

Trust forms the foundation for a more constructive approach to organizational rules. In order to foster trust, policies must demonstrate an expectation of trustworthy behavior on the part of organizational participants, as well as be responsive to breaches of trust (Coleman, 1990). Sanctions that punish those who violate trust have the effect of constraining employee behavior within acceptable bounds. A leader must also have the courage to exercise these controls, since trust is supported by credible, but relatively unused, threats and sanctions (Lindskold & Bennett, 1973).

At Brookside, there was a strong sense of accountability, but there was also more flexibility and leniency for the unexpected ups and downs of life. When there was a sense of confidence that teachers were working hard and going beyond their minimum commitments, there was a greater willingness to make allowances for teachers. For example, a teacher might be dismissed early to see his or her own child's school program or take a child to the orthodontist. Teachers responded by making sure they were worthy of the trust placed in them. They described a sense of urgency to get back after an illness, knowing their absence was placing a burden on colleagues. Instead of minimum compliance, they went beyond the requirements of their contract and district policies. A culture of distrust is likely to hamper a school's ability to be productive, whereas trust can pay off for schools in giving them the flexibility to respond to the needs of their clients, staff, and community.

Putting It into Action

If you enter a school or a district that is characterized by a culture of control, you will need to take deliberate steps to begin to foster a culture of trust. If you assume the leadership of a school that is encumbered by an overabundance of rules, it may help to reframe the rules as parameters for behavior. In the school I led in a low-income neighborhood of Chicago, we learned that you can never specify all of the behaviors that are not allowed; there will always be those students who use their creativity to find the loopholes in the system. An alternative is to specify broad parameters that articulate the character we hope for in our collective life. In our school, we had just three school rules: *This is a safe place; this is a caring place; this is a learning place.* We began each school year with a discussion in which we brainstormed or imagined different kinds of actions and whether they fell within or outside the parameters we had set. This helped our students begin to learn to exercise judgment in response to particular situations. These three rules were bolstered by procedures, such as how to line up for lunch, where to put the materials away at the end of a lesson, or how to indicate a desire to speak during a class discussion. The parameters apply equally to teacher behavior, and in a school that has tolerated bad behavior on the part of teachers as well as students, it may take time, patience, and persistence to make it clear that the rules apply to everyone.

You need to demonstrate a commitment to the rules and policies of your school and district and a willingness to deal with those who violate them. However, you can also demonstrate flexibility and a willingness to bend the rules occasionally when a teacher has a valid need. Rather than laxness, a practice of *strategic leniency* is more likely to generate trust by balancing a commitment to fair procedures and a commitment to people.

Key Points About Revenge and a Culture of Control

- Revenge may be useful in equalizing the power within organizations and opening the possibility for constructive change.

- There is a motivation for revenge when the victim perceives malevolence or self-interest on the part of the perpetrator.

- Resentment tends to be clandestine and defensive in nature, thus making the restoration of trust more difficult.

- Micromanagement is an act of distrust and is likely to lead to resentment.

- A breakdown in trust leads to a proliferation of rules, which can hamper school effectiveness.

- As professionals, teachers need trust and discretion in order to be responsive to the needs of their clients, the students.

Questions for Reflection and Discussion

1. Is there a culture of control evident at your school? What could you do to replace this mentality with a more trusting one?

2. Do the rules in your school serve it well or poorly? Do they reflect a culture of trust or distrust?

3. When have you seen resentment lead to sabotage?

6

Teachers Trusting One Another

It is an equal failing to trust everybody, and to trust nobody.

English proverb

Professional learning communities share three important features: the adults in them act and are treated as professionals, there is a focus on learning, and there is a strong sense of community. For these three features to characterize a school's culture, trust is required. In turn, the culture of a school plays a significant role in supporting and sustaining trust. The actions of the principal play an important role in setting the general tone of school trust, but teacher behavior has a more direct impact on student learning. Teachers are more likely to be innovative and effective in an atmosphere of trust.

Strong professional communities are built through joint deliberation and decision making. Fullan (2003) argues for the importance of "disciplined, informed professional inquiry" (p. 11) in bringing about constructive school change. This inquiry is supported by standards of professionalism, as well as norms of curiosity. Professional learning communities are based on trust that teachers and principals will act with the best interests of students in mind by researching best practices and pursuing data to bolster decision making (Elmore, Peterson, & McCarthey, 1996; Goldring & Rallis, 1993; Louis et al., 1996).

Professional learning communities are characterized by the quality, tone, and content of the dialogue among the professionals. Principals can influence this dialogue by the example they set. The principal can also create time and structures that facilitate collaboration and that allow for professional discourse and shared decision making among the teachers. The principal can foster openness by encouraging teachers to be in one another's classrooms, observe one another teaching, and give constructive feedback. Establishing a peer observation program takes planning and training to build the kind of safety and trust that teachers need for a program of this kind to be successful.

An atmosphere of trust holds promise for transforming schools into vibrant learning communities. To foster the kinds of support teachers need for risk taking and professional growth, they need trust. Cultural norms in a professional learning community can facilitate trust by encouraging a culture of cooperation rather than cutthroat competition. A cooperative culture is likely to have a significant impact on the trusting and trustworthy behavior of not only teachers and staff, but of students as well (Louis et al., 1995; Tschannen-Moran, 2001). Building a culture of trust in schools may require time, effort, and leadership, but the investment is likely to bring satisfying returns.

Building a Professional Community at Brookside

Things didn't start out easily for Brenda at Brookside. When she had assumed leadership nearly a decade earlier, the school was embroiled in conflict. Discipline was inconsistent and largely ineffective. The quality of teaching was far below what she would have hoped to see. It took time and patience to begin to shape the school into a professional learning community. She described her first year: "My first year was difficult. I learned very quickly that I could not expect to have an open discussion with the full staff. Their meetings had been characterized by conflict. I held team meetings regularly for the first couple of years, saving full staff meetings only for one-way communication. I listened a lot. I sent out weekly memos as a way of organizing the school, keeping everybody up to speed, and expressing appreciation. The staff let me know they appreciated this regular communication."

Part of Brenda's challenge was in changing the culture of the school, especially the proprietary feelings teachers' had over their classrooms. They valued privacy and autonomy, and were guarded in their protectiveness of that space. Brenda challenged those norms from the very beginning, and she did so with a combination of strength and sensitivity. She described the initial reaction from teachers:

> On the first day of school I visited every classroom. I continued to visit each classroom every day the first week of school just for short visits to get a feel for the building and to be visible. Early the next week I was visited by a teacher who spoke for herself and "others" and explained to me that it was not the practice of that building for the principal to visit classrooms without an appointment. I explained that I could not make good decisions for the school community without being in classrooms and suggested she pass the word. I showed her the list I had made of things that I could do to improve the learning environment, things like repair of clocks, moving old books, etc. That changed her attitude.

Over time Brenda was able to improve the quality of teaching through an artful combination of support and challenge. Brenda's affirmation and acceptance of differences in teaching style helped created an atmosphere where teachers were willing to share with one another. Christy described how Brenda's leadership helped shape the culture at the school:

Our principal is very sensitive to everyone's differences. But then she plays on our strengths within our differences and she treats all of us equally. There is nobody who is put up on a pedestal at any time. That's something that changes the whole atmosphere between staff members because you never have that sense of competition. If you need help in something you feel comfortable going to your coworkers and asking for help—or sharing what has worked for you or what hasn't worked for you. It is never an embarrassing situation. Brenda will point things out, but she doesn't do it in a way that makes anyone feel inferior because she always brings out that person's strength. That person's strength may not be your strength so you don't take offense at it. But the next conversation you may be the person whose strengths she may be discussing. Every person feels valued.

Without a sense of competition or the need to protect one's turf, these teachers were able to benefit from one another's expertise and ideas.

Brenda encountered a school culture that was not only divided by conflict, but was also one in which teachers had adopted an individualistic, "every person for himself" orientation. One of the ways that the negative culture at Brookside was evidenced was in the hoarding of supplies.

All the returning teachers had placed art orders the previous year. They tucked those materials in their cupboards. The rooms of the new staff were empty of art materials. I entered rooms over the weekend and borrowed from Peter to pay Paul, so to speak. The scarcity of construction paper and art materials became a symbol for me of the general view that there was a scarcity of everything, like appreciation for teachers and praise for students. I put up shelves in a closet, purchased new materials, and announced that teachers could take what they needed. The closet was empty within a few days so I reordered enough times to refill the closet and see materials remain until needed rather than being hoarded.

One of the ways that Brenda communicated her concern for the well-being of the teachers as she began to overcome the sense of scarcity was to keep a bottomless jar of candy in the teachers' lounge. Over time, this became a clever device that Brenda used as a barometer to assess the stress level in the school. "I kept a jar of candy in the teachers' lounge. I could measure the stress level of the staff by the consumption of candy. Generally speaking, there was some candy left in the jar at the end of the day on Monday and Tuesday, but on Friday I refilled the jar at least once. It was usually empty by 10:00 A.M. on Fridays and at report card time or other times of stress. I learned not to introduce new ideas or duties when the candy jar was most active."

Brenda wanted to find a way to bolster the sense of community in the school and move away from teachers' more individualistic orientation. She struck upon a school play as an avenue for doing so. But implementing her idea didn't turn out to be easy.

I felt that it would be good for the school community if we had a schoolwide performance, and I asked the music teacher how she felt about doing one. She said she was not willing to put that much time into her job at this time of her life. The assistant principal had informed me that she did not like to handle discipline (and she didn't do an especially good job at it either). She was, however, quite creative and she readily agreed to visit classrooms, do language experience writing, and write a school play—which turned out to be very clever. It was a major production and accomplished just what I hoped for in building a sense of community with parents, students, and staff. I couldn't help but be amused at the end of the school year when the music teacher told me that she should have been the one giving that play. I reminded her of our conversation, and she was surprised that she had responded in that manner. The next year she put on a schoolwide play.

The transformation of Brookside into a professional learning community did not happen overnight. It took several years of steady progress toward that goal. Once teachers learned that they could trust Brenda and her intentions for them, they began to be willing to take risks and try new teaching techniques. Team meetings grew to be times of true collaboration rather than complaint sessions. Teachers were more willing to invest the extra effort required of excellent teaching and bring more creativity and imagination to their work lives. Bolstered by a strong sense of community, they increased their commitment to the students and the school.

Faculty Trust in Colleagues

When members of the school community interact in a cordial way, they establish a feeling and appearance that everything is normal and in proper order, and this feeling helps create a context in which trust is more likely to develop (Lewis & Weigert, 1985). The professional norms at Brookside encourage teachers to interact frequently in face-to-face, positive ways and assist one another in their work with students.

Whether or not teachers trust one another can have a significant impact on the climate and effectiveness of a school. A collegial atmosphere, authentic relationships, and the level of involvement of teachers in decision making all play a major role in faculty trust in colleagues (Tarter, Bliss, & Hoy, 1989; Tarter, Sabo, & Hoy, 1995;

Tschannen-Moran & Hoy, 1998). Teacher morale is strongly related to faculty trust in colleagues as well. High trust in colleagues creates a context for positive morale, and where distrust is pervasive, morale can be expected to be low (Smith, Hoy, & Sweetland, 2001).

All five facets of trust are important in teachers' trust judgments of colleagues. A sense of benevolence or caring lays a foundation of trust among teachers. Honesty, openness, and reliability also played a role. An interesting pattern of trust emerges, however, when teachers lack respect for the competence of their colleagues.

Benevolence

A sense of caring or benevolence was the single most often mentioned dimension of faculty trust in their colleagues. At Brookside, teachers expressed support for one another in a variety of ways across both the professional and personal realms of life, from helping new teachers get started to taking hot meals to a staff member who was ill. Kathy described how welcome the other teachers had made her feel when she arrived at Brookside: "My very first year, one of the fourth grade teachers was constantly giving me things, saying, 'Here's an idea.' She did my first three days of lesson plans for me. She said 'Here, here's an outline for you. If you like it, use it, if you don't, don't.' Just because she knew I was going to struggle. Like those flowers (pointing to a vase on her desk), she just sent flowers around the building to brighten everybody's day. Just because. She just wants people to feel good. That's her way of keeping everybody smiling."

Christy, another Brookside teacher, echoed the ways that veteran faculty welcomed and looked out for new teachers, even when the newcomers had previous teaching experience: "They help new people coming in by—when an extra expectation is due, they might say, 'You know what? You're new. I'm going to take your class for an hour and why don't you work on your writing portfolios.' Just because they know that the first year you have a lot of extra training and that is all on your own personal time—and it is a lot. The principal doesn't say, 'Go and do this.' They just do it on their own. It is a wonderful working environment. It balances out the hard work."

A spirit of cooperation lays a foundation for trust to develop, and greater trust helps create greater cooperation. The tradition at Brookside of cooperative and helpful behavior toward new teachers helped create the conditions for trust to develop. Once trust is established, those novice teachers are more likely to behave in cooperative ways, and the cycle of trust is likely to become self-sustaining.

In addition to help at school, Brookside teachers exhibited a particular pride in the ways the faculty looked out for one another beyond the bounds of their work life. Kathy continued:

> We have collected money at Christmastime to give to people because they are struggling a little bit financially. There are people who have gone through divorces and the staff has known about that and they have helped deal with that. We have a staff member who was diagnosed with cancer and every Monday they would take dinner over to the family. When a staff member had used all of her sick leave, we donated our sick leave so that she could continue to stay out. We are very caring. Whenever there is a tragedy that has happened in someone's life and we know about that, then we respond. As well as exciting events like pregnancies and marriages— we buy gifts and go and attend.

David, another teacher at Brookside, explained how the atmosphere of caring contributed to a sense of community: "You want to have that sense of belonging. And you want others to belong. Just knowing that you're missed when you're not here—it makes you feel good." The overarching ethos of caring not only made for a more pleasant work environment, it created the context for the development of trust throughout the school community.

Honesty

At Brookside, the teachers took for granted the honesty and integrity of their colleagues. Integrity is demonstrated by doing what you say you will, telling the truth, and keeping promises. Authenticity, or being "real," accepting responsibility and avoiding shifting blame for errors to others, has been found to be significantly related to teacher trust in colleagues (Hoy & Kupersmith, 1985; Tschannen-Moran & Hoy, 1998). For example, a teacher at Lincoln forfeited the trust of her colleagues when she attempted to dodge Gloria's tongue-lashing by pointing fingers at her teammates when she was the one who had dropped the ball in preparing for a field trip, a mistake that resulted in last-minute transportation problems.

The effects of a betrayal are not just intense, they are also lasting. Paul, a teacher at Fremont, described a breach of civic order in a situation in which a fellow teacher intentionally distorted the facts in order to put Paul in a bad light with Fred. As part of a class assignment, Paul had invited some of his university classmates to engage in a discussion with several Fremont faculty members about the strengths and weaknesses of the professional development activities in the school. Fred was scheduled to be a part of the discussion but at the last minute was unable to attend. One of the teachers who had participated in the session called Fred at home that evening to report on the event. The day after the meeting, Paul was called to come to Fred's office. Paul described his chagrin at what happened: "Fred said, 'I heard you all tore me apart yesterday.' I was taken aback and I said, 'Fred, what do you mean?' I said, 'No, I have the session taped if you want to listen to the tape recording.' That person who'd made the call was the main person who had criticized him! That was real hard to deal with. That's the first time I ever had an administrator call me in his office and shut the door. And I'm thinking, 'I don't know what I did wrong!'"

Based on the strong personal relationship Paul had with Fred, and bolstered by the evidence of the tape recording, they were able to work through the misunderstanding and repair their relationship. It seemed evident that the perpetrator thought she could gain an advantage by causing Fred to distrust Paul. Although the rift with Fred was repaired, Paul refused to speak to the colleague who had made the call and avoided any social contact with her. He continued to maintain his silence more than a year after the incident.

Openness

At Brookside, teachers are pleased to share professional secrets, successful teaching strategies, materials, and equipment in the interests of helping students learn. A spirit of openness allows for greater sharing of both ideas and resources (Kratzer, 1997; Short & Greer, 1997). Openness fosters trust but also grows out of a high level of trust; it is part of the spiral of trust. Kathy described the openness to sharing ideas at Brookside:

> We go to each other for advice on a lesson or if we need resources. We're not afraid to ask other teachers. We'll even go observe other teachers during our specials so we can see what techniques they're using that we can learn. There's an openness. The teachers don't look at you like, "Why are you walking into my room?" We can just walk in each other's room freely and if there is something I want, like the overhead projector or whatever, I can just take it, and they can do the same. There is just that sense of trust that it won't be abused, and it will be returned.

Brookside teachers also didn't feel threatened by others giving them ideas or offering suggestions. Christy elaborated: "We might say, 'What's that I see you hanging outside? That's really neat, can we do it? Do you have extra copies? How did that work?' Or you might go over and say, 'I tried this today and the kids really liked it. You might want to try it with your class.' If something worked and your children really benefited from it, why wouldn't you want as many children as possible to gain from that? I think everyone thinks that way."

Knowledge (particularly if it is hard to come by) is a source of power (Jones & George, 1998). In an environment of trust, people are more likely to be open with information because they feel more confident that others will not exploit the information for their own benefit.

There was not only an openness with teaching ideas and strategies at Brookside, but also in sharing personal information. Teachers were willing to share things that were near to their hearts: concerns and joys about family, friends, and life outside of school. With this sharing came vulnerability that the information would be misused in ways that were hurtful. Although teachers at Brookside acknowledged that word about one another was likely to spread quickly, there was a sense of confidence that whatever information people received about one another would be handled with care. The pervasive atmosphere of trust enabled teachers and staff members to ask about and share things that in another context might be a problem or cause discomfort. David explained: "When you trust other teachers and you know they trust you, you feel comfortable. When they ask about things, you don't feel like they are dipping into your business. You are just happy to talk about it."

At both Lincoln and Fremont, teachers were much more reluctant to be open in both the personal and professional realms. Paul explained that at Fremont he had learned through hard experience to be guarded about sharing information about his life outside of school: "The gossip runs rampant here. It spreads very fast. The best thing I have done—if I have a bit of news that's concerning me or somebody else, I keep it to myself. I don't tell anybody. If I have a problem with me, I keep it to myself. Because if you tell just one person, they'll all know. It's like playing telephone, where you tell one person, and it gets totally distorted by the time it gets around."

This lack of openness was linked to a concern about the level of benevolence or good will Paul could count on from his peers. Without the confidence that others would respond in a caring manner, there was a reluctance to make himself vulnerable through the sharing of information about things that were important to him.

A frequently mentioned breach in the civic order among teachers was the breaking of confidences. Mary, a teacher at Lincoln School, described an incident of betrayal through the breaking of her confidence by another teacher. Mary had been pressured by Gloria to serve on a particular committee, which put her in an awkward position because she didn't want it to be known that she was interviewing for positions at other schools. She confided in Leslie, the alternate to the committee, that she might need to call on her from time to time if her interview schedule conflicted with the committee meetings. One afternoon, Mary walked into a classroom to overhear Leslie telling another teacher about Mary's plans to interview elsewhere. The other teacher was a close confidant of Gloria, so Mary knew Gloria would soon be made aware of her plans. Mary described how the scenario unfolded: "I walked in and heard her. Leslie knew that that person would communicate with Gloria. When I walked in, she walked out and didn't make eye contact. I called her on it though. I confronted her."

Allisha, another Lincoln teacher, described what happened when it was discovered that a colleague had made a habit of breaking confidences. Allisha explained how the teacher involved felt the collective wrath of a group of teachers whose confidence she had betrayed: "There is one teacher who likes to talk about everyone in the building. She and I started together last year, and I really confided in her. But one teacher came and told everyone what she had been saying. Come to find out she basically just repeated everything I had said. So we just snub her. When she tries to talk to people, they just basically turn away or change the subject. She got the message that she wasn't welcome."

So openness needs to be tempered with good judgment and care. But a lack of openness can provoke a downward spiral of distrust. Without openness, teachers do not have the opportunity to demonstrate benevolence, reliability, and competence to one another.

Reliability

Teachers talked about the importance of being able to depend on other teachers to live up to their commitments or take their responsibilities seriously. Being able to count on colleagues in the midst of unexpected circumstances was important to teachers. Kathy described the sense of responsibility teachers at Brookside felt to one another in emergencies: "We take each other's kids a lot. Nobody ever says no. The day I had to do that I gave everybody candy bars in appreciation. But they said, "You didn't have to do that, that is just the Brookside way." There is a high level of trust that people will be here unless they are dead on their feet or seriously ill. They won't abandon their room or stick somebody else with it. If emergencies arise, if one person has to leave because their son or daughter is ill, teachers will automatically take over their students."

One of the ways that people help build and sustain a sense of trust in the collective is "compensatory trust," whereby people cover for one another when they become aware that someone may have dropped the ball (Kramer et al., 1996). David reported his confidence in his colleagues' dependability, as well as how compensatory trust was at work at Brookside: "Off the top of my head, I just can't recall an instance when someone was supposed to have done something and didn't. There is a high degree of professionalism here, and they are committed to what it is they are doing. When they say something, I think they have every intention of following through with that. What I have seen is where others kind of pick up where the other person should have been. Other people fill in. But usually when people have made the commitment to do something they follow through with it." Teachers need to feel that they can rely on their colleagues if trust is to develop.

In schools where reliability was absent, teachers grew to distrust their colleagues. At Fremont, teachers were much less confident that colleagues would show up where they were supposed to or would step into the gap for one another. Kelli had given up trying to ensure that there would be adequate supervision at recess. Teachers might be reliable as far as other teachers within their clique, but not necessarily to the students or the school program as a whole.

Competence

When it comes to teachers' trust in one another, the issue of competence is not a simple one. The degree to which competence matters to teachers' trust in one another is related to how interdependent they feel in the teaching realm. In some cases, this perception was in flux because of the pressures placed on the school due to the accountability movement, or in other cases, by moves toward more team teaching. As perceptions of interdependence increased, judgments of one another's competence became a more salient part of teachers' trust in colleagues. Principals can influence the degree of interdependence teachers perceive in how they talk about and structure the school program.

Assessments of colleagues' competence were influenced by teaching philosophy and style. One pair of teachers who had begun the first tentative moves toward teaming was struggling over issues of teaching philosophy and style. One teacher took pride in having maintained an active schedule of professional development and reading and in using the most up-to-date teaching methods, whereas her partner employed much more traditional teaching methods. In addition to the difference in philosophy, these two teachers came from different racial groups, which compounded the challenge of working through differences. Nonetheless, both teachers felt there would be benefits for their students, as well as themselves, in sharing classes for certain subjects, so they committed to working through the difficulties. This required a deeper level of trust than had been necessary in the many previous years of teaching across the same hall from one another.

Understanding teachers' trust in their colleagues is further complicated by evidence of uneven trust, that is, teachers felt they could trust one another in some arenas and not in others. Teachers drew distinctions between professional and personal trust, suggesting that there were two sets of expectations about what teachers believed they owed one another: what they felt they owed to one another as professional colleagues and what they owed one another as friends and fellow human beings. When teachers did not hold the professional competence of their colleagues in high regard, they were nonetheless able to justify their trust by distinguishing personal trust from professional trust. Although there was overlap, these two kinds of trust seemed to be somewhat independent from each other. Rob, a Lincoln teacher, described the distinction this way:

> Personally, I would trust any faculty member here with anything, whether it be taking my car, house sitting, anything. . . . As far as the professional aspect, I feel some people don't live up to their end of the deal. In past years, when I taught in the upper grades, I saw children who came to me who were not prepared. I have a feeling it is due to some of the professional qualities of some of the people I work with. I don't hold that against them personally, but I feel that there could be a little more dedication among the staff members.

Paul made a similar distinction between professional and personal trust at Fremont, but reported that he held higher professional trust than personal trust:

> I think there are two different levels. The professional deals with any issues or concerns at the school level. I think there is a high level of trust here because everybody

values each other's opinions. I think there is another level that surfaces among faculty that deals with the interpersonal relationships that teachers have that have nothing to do with the school per se. There may be outside influences like church, or it may be sororities they once belonged to, or they may have taught together for a long time. That level of trust can create a barrier. There's a lot of gossip that will go around which is not really professional gossip; it may be personal gossip. That creates mistrust.

In Paul's view, a high level of personal trust within subgroups or cliques impaired the development of an overall sense of trust among the faculty as a whole. Fred's failure to intervene to help resolve conflicts or to enforce norms of behavior allowed the sense of community within the faculty to become fragmented and to deteriorate.

Some teachers believed that their interdependence with other teachers centered on issues of reliability in facilitating the processes that kept the school running smoothly, not necessarily on others' skill in the classroom. Paul reported that he did not feel that judgments about whether colleagues were doing a good job in the classroom entered into his calculation of professional trust because he did not feel that their classroom performance had an impact on him professionally. He said: "I have seen teachers that a lot of people felt were incompetent or really shouldn't have been teaching. I think the trust was there but I don't think we as educators took that trust to mean that we are trusting them because they are competent or not competent. We're trusting them because they do help the smooth running of the school. But, to me, competence and incompetence, that's another issue. Now if we were teaming, that would affect me. But we are so isolated right now that it doesn't affect me."

Paul acknowledged that if he felt dependent on another teacher's skill, if it affected him because of a situation of interdependence, then a colleague's professional competence might be of concern. However, he did not perceive that level of interdependence. Some teachers did perceive interdependence, though, and did feel that their colleague's competence mattered. Brian said that he did not trust one of his

> I HAVE A colleague who came right out and said, "I don't like boys." As the mother of two sons, I lost all professional respect for her that day.
>
> *Beth, third grade teacher*

colleagues, in part, because of the disrespectful tone toward her students that he overheard as he passed by her classroom. This disrespect affected both his personal and professional trust of that person.

Each of the five facets of trust contributed to teachers' trust in one another, although the picture was complicated when it came to judgments of competence. As long as teachers were not dependent on the teaching competence of their colleagues, they were able to foster trusting relationships with colleagues in spite of negative assessments of their colleagues' teaching abilities. But with greater schoolwide accountability, the competence of one's colleagues is likely to become more salient in trust judgments. The level of trust among the faculty of a school has very real consequences for how the school functions and its ability to meet its goals. In the next section, we will explore some of the important school dynamics that are related to the level of faculty trust, the level of collaboration, the collective sense of efficacy, and the constructive resolution of conflict.

The Payoffs of Faculty Trust

Trust plays an important role in overcoming barriers to building a professional learning community, including conflict avoidance, destructive competitiveness, and low levels of teacher efficacy (Leonard, 1999). The payoffs of a high level of faculty trust are many. These include the facilitation of greater collaboration, a more robust collective sense among teachers that they can make a difference, and more productive conflict resolution strategies.

Fluid Collaboration

Greater collaboration among teachers fosters a spirit of professional community in schools, but such collaboration is unlikely to develop in the absence of trust among teachers. Statistical analyses across a large number of schools reflect the patterns that we see at Brookside, Lincoln, and Fremont (Tschannen-Moran, 2001). In schools where there was greater trust, there tended to be a greater level of collaboration. When trust was absent, people were reluctant to work closely together, and collaboration was more difficult.

When trust was high and teachers felt affirmed by their principal, they were much more willing to make themselves vulnerable through teamwork and sharing with other teachers. The spirit of collaboration at Brookside translated into classroom practice, not only in the frequent use of group work in class activities and a conscious step-by-step process for resolving interpersonal difficulties among students, but also in a program in which older students teamed up with younger students to read and do projects. Teachers saw this program as helping older students polish their own skills as they used them to instruct the younger students. The younger students benefited from the one-on-one attention of an older friend. Christy described the positive dynamics she observed: "Buddies are very much an integral part of our curriculum, doing cross-grade-level things. We have a class that we work with and we may write stories with them, we may do art projects with them, we may write books with them. At the beginning of the year, my students read to the younger students but by this time in the year they read to us. And my kids love it. They'll say, 'Hey! This kid's reading at such-and-such a level!' or 'They're a good writer!' That creates part of the sense of community too."

Teachers saw this program as beneficial not only for the younger students but for the older ones as well. Upper grade students who had struggled with schoolwork themselves took pride in the accomplishments of their younger buddies and became more engaged learners. These positive outcomes would not be possible if the teachers did not trust each other enough to collaborate on the planning and implementation of this program.

The spirit of teamwork and cooperation at Brookside did not just happen by accident. There was evidence of hard work and a conscious effort toward making it happen. This effort began with the vision the principal articulated for the school and the resources she made available to make it a reality. The dividends were clear. Teachers, students, and parents benefited from the strong sense of community that resulted.

At Lincoln, teachers cut corners on planning and meeting with other teachers, and they did not extend themselves for each other in the way that the teachers at Brookside reported. Mary, a veteran teacher at Lincoln, described her disappointment at the lack of willingness of her colleagues to share ideas or to try new things.

> I would like to see more sharing going on—an openness that is not quite there throughout the whole staff. If you throw out an idea, it's not like, "Well, let's consider it. What are the strengths? What are the weaknesses?" It's not really analyzed. It's like, "I just don't have the time." I've always been someone who is willing to put in the time and so I feel kind of resentful. I have put in a lot

---

WE HAVE TWENTY-FIVE regular education students and six deaf students in our room. Some teachers are not willing to do this inclusion thing. They want to do things their own way, to make decisions their own way. They are not willing to let someone in to work with them. They don't want to be critically analyzed. On the other hand, there are real advantages to having two people in the room. It is easier in a lot of ways. Two bodies are better than one when you have discipline problems. You can take phone calls. You can go to the bathroom. It's a lot more fun to plan together, to come up with some really good things together. You feel more like a team.

Tracy, first grade teacher

of time and no one is willing to put forth the effort. That's across the board. I think the children go above and beyond, but the adults don't.

When the sharing of ideas was not reciprocated within teams of teachers, it led to resentment. Mary continued: "There is a teacher who is leaving her position here because the other teachers she works with always look to her to do the work—to do the planning and finding resources. When she shares, she expects them to share, and they never share with her. Then when she doesn't do it for them, they get upset."

An obstacle to collaboration among teachers is that autonomy is strongly ingrained in the teaching profession. This dynamic was particularly pronounced at Fremont. Reluctance to give up autonomy was cited as a reason for the difficulty of making collaboration work. In addition to the fear of losing autonomy, teachers also were reluctant to expose themselves to the scrutiny and possible criticism of their peers. Paul explained:

> We talked about peer observation. We even made a schedule where there would be peer coaching among the teams and we would take over their class. But they wouldn't do it. We tried videotape. Boy, did they buck on that! Because they had to critique them after they watched them. Everybody is in their private domain and they want to protect that. We have an open-door policy. The doors are not allowed to be shut in the building: anybody can come in. But once you try to set something up where people can observe another colleague, they are not very receptive to it.

One reason Paul saw for this resistance was that a number of teachers liked to gain status by talking as though they were doing a lot of innovative things in their classrooms when in reality their teaching remained very traditional.

Teachers may not only be reluctant to collaborate themselves, they may also feel threatened when others in their schools begin to collaborate. They may communicate this discomfort through social sanctions, as Brian learned to his dismay. Brian, a novice fourth grade teacher at Fremont, began to collaborate with Kelli, an experienced first grade teacher, by setting up a "reading buddies" mentoring program between the two classes. They also tried collaborating in other subject areas. Brian described what happened: "This fall, Kelli and I had our classes working together studying trees and fall leaves. That was pretty cool. We were able to mix up both the primary and the intermediate. We took our classes out to some of the parks near here. But then the other teachers asked me bluntly was I having an affair with her! They were joking, I think, but they were also half serious. That really upset me!" As a married man and the father of young children, Brian was deeply hurt by this treatment. He felt that his attempts to work with another teacher were not only noticed but disapproved of by the other members of the faculty. He was put on notice that that kind of teamwork was not welcomed. Brian was disappointed that Fred did not step in to support this cross–grade level collaboration.

Robust Collective Efficacy

When teachers trust each other, it is more likely that they will develop greater confidence in their collective ability to be successful at meeting their goals. This collective sense of efficacy is related to greater motivation toward the accomplishment of the goals of the school, greater effort, and greater persistence in the face of setbacks.

The idea that what people believe about their ability to be successful at the task at hand can make a difference to their motivation and actual achievement falls under the label of "self-efficacy beliefs" (Bandura, 1997). There is a large body of research that demonstrates that what teachers as individuals believe about the extent to which they can influence the learning and achievement of their students makes a significant difference in their teaching behaviors and outcomes (Tschannen-Moran, Woolfolk Hoy, & Hoy, 1998). Teachers with stronger efficacy beliefs are likely to be more enthusiastic, more organized, and devote more time in planning their teaching (Allinder, 1994). In addition, teachers with a stronger sense that they can successfully affect student learning are less likely to become angry, impatient, or frustrated with a student who is having difficulty; will stick with that student longer; and will try more strategies to help the student understand (Ashton & Webb, 1986; Gibson & Dembo, 1984). Thus, teachers' sense of efficacy exerts significant influence on student achievement by promoting teacher behaviors that enhance learning. Indeed, higher teacher efficacy has been shown to be positively related to higher student achievement (Anderson, Greene, & Loewen, 1988; Armor et al., 1976; Ashton & Webb, 1986; Ross, 1992).

Beliefs can be shared by the faculty as a whole and can help explain group behavior and group outcomes (Bandura, 1993, 1997; Sampson, Raudenbush, & Felton, 1997). These shared beliefs are evidenced in the norms of a school and the small talk concerning expectations about the likelihood of success of a school faculty. Collective teacher efficacy refers to the perceptions of teachers in a school that the efforts of the faculty as a whole will have positive effects on students. Teachers and schools are more likely to persist in efforts that support goals that they believe they can accomplish.

Principals can help to cultivate and nourish strong collective efficacy beliefs through communicating confidence in the ability of teachers to promote student learning, whatever the difficulties and challenges of the particular context of the school. Teachers' collective sense of efficacy has been linked to student achievement, even when taking into account the socioeconomic status of students (Bandura, 1993; Goddard, Hoy, & Woolfolk Hoy, 2001; Tschannen-

Moran & Barr, 2004). This collective sense of being able to successfully fulfill the mission of the school has also been linked to teachers' trust in one another as well as to teachers' trust in students and parents (Goddard, Tschannen-Moran, & Hoy, 2001). When a high level of trust prevails in a school, a sense of collective efficacy tends to be evident as well. There was a rise in the collective sense of efficacy among the teachers at Brookside as their level of trust increased and they grew into a professional learning community. Trust bolstered the risk taking of new teaching practice, which was rewarded with higher student achievement, which in turn raised the sense that the teachers could make a difference even among their most disadvantaged students.

Constructive Controversy

One of the primary causes of the disruption of trust in schools is conflict that has been handled poorly. People are in conflict when the actions of one person are perceived as interfering, obstructing, or in some other way making another's behavior less effective (Tjosvold, 1997). Conflict can be thought of as a struggle between interdependent parties who perceive incompatible goals, scarce resources and rewards, and potential interference from the other party in achieving their goals (Baron, 1997; Hocker & Wilmot, 1985; Rubin, Pruit, & Kim, 1994).

How individuals respond to conflict can either foster trust or damage it. People make choices in how they respond to conflict, sometimes consciously and thoughtfully, other times reacting in the heat of the moment out of fear and anger. Deutsch (2000) organized these common responses across six continua that reflect a number of choices people make in response to conflict.

- Along the first continuum, people at one extreme tend
  to avoid conflict (denying, suppressing, or postponing
  it) whereas at the other extreme they confront it,

involving themselves in order to demonstrate their confidence and courage in the face of conflict. Within schools, Peterson and Peterson (1990) found both children and adults employed conflict avoidance twice as often as confrontation.

- The second set of responses Deutsch characterized as being along the spectrum from hard to soft; that is, participants respond in an aggressive, unyielding fashion at one extreme or they may be excessively gentle and unassertive at the other.

- A third continuum of choice runs between rigid and loose responses; people may attempt to organize or control the situation, on the one hand, or lean toward avoiding all formal responses, on the other.

- Yet another continuum spans the divide between intellectual and affective responses to conflict in that some individuals may respond to conflict with calm detachment whereas others may express intense emotions.

- Individuals at one end of the fifth continuum may attempt to escalate the conflict, expressing it in its largest possible terms, whereas at the other extreme individuals seek to minimize the seriousness of the differences between themselves and others.

- Finally, in attempts to communicate with others about the difficulties at hand, disputants at one end of the continuum will choose bluntness, revealing all they think and feel, whereas disputants at the other end will hold their cards close, concealing what is on their mind.

The tone and style of approaching and handling conflict will be defined along these six continua. Individuals' history and biases regarding conflict affect their responses. As individuals continue to engage in conflict, learning new strategies for productive resolutions, the range of possible responses is extended and enriched.

In schools, teachers often respond to conflict either by acting aggressively to try to force their will on others or by avoiding or suppressing conflict because they fear the consequences will be uncontrollable. This avoidance may stem from a lack of skills and confidence to manage the conflict constructively. Schools can reap the benefits of constructive controversy by understanding common responses to conflict and by supporting teachers and other members of the school community toward using conflict strategies that lead to constructive outcomes. The principal can play an important role in helping to mediate between the two parties who are in conflict, as well as ensure that disputants guard against personal attacks and threats. Schools as professional learning communities can benefit by improving the conflict resolution skills of members of that community by fostering lively debate over differences in ideas and strongly held positions about what should be done. Schools with faculty who have these skills will reap better quality decisions and improved group functioning (Uline et al., 2003).

Once teachers at Brookside gained better conflict management skills, these skills became an accepted part of the school culture, a taken-for-granted sense of "how we do things around here." The teachers became invested in this more constructive way of managing their collective lives. Brenda recalled: "Teachers were surprised to be reminded later of the behavior they exhibited while they were in the conflict situation. They were so embroiled in their hurt feelings or inability to be productive that they didn't see what was going on around them. One teacher actually told me that it was an adult conflict and had

WE WERE TRYING to resolve a dispute at a faculty meeting, and one of my colleagues just deteriorated into street talk. It was very unprofessional. I have never trusted her since that time. I just keep my distance.

Melody, special education teacher

no effect on the students. They could not recognize the environment as the negative force that it was."

When teachers in a school do not trust one another, they are likely to be guarded in their interactions. Energy is diverted from common goals and channeled into self-protection. Collaboration deteriorates. Teachers may go through the motions of grade-level or department meetings, but there is little real joint decision making or collaboration. Teachers' collective sense that they have what it takes to promote student learning is reduced when distrust overtakes a school and motivation consequently suffers. Schools fraught with poorly handled conflict are likely to suffer from lower trust. The processes involved are reciprocal, resulting in a spiral of distrust. Greater collaboration, stronger collective sense of efficacy, and constructive conflict resolution are more likely when trust is present; however, they also foster the conditions that make for greater trust.

Putting It into Action

Although teachers' trust in their colleagues stems directly from teachers' behavior and not from the behavior of the principal, there is much that you can do to foster a professional learning community based in trust. One of the most important things that you can do is to be explicit in establishing the norms as to how teachers treat one another and then address breaches of this agreement forthrightly. Enforce positive norms of conduct and promote and defend the norms that support professional engagement. This takes sensitivity and courage, but without a defender, the culture is likely to tolerate behavior that is destructive to a productive sense of community. Being available to mediate conflicts and, over time, helping teachers gain the skills to resolve conflicts constructively themselves will go a long way toward bolstering the level of trust among faculty.

Schools get the teachers they deserve. Rather than starting from a position of blame when teachers do not initially meet the standards of professional performance you would like, it is more constructive to assume that, at least in part, people are behaving the way they are in response to their environment. Organizational cultures emerge as a pattern of shared assumptions that a group has learned in response to the problems they have encountered collectively, and that are then taught to new members as the correct way to perceive, think, and feel in relation to those problems (Schein, 1992). To change a distrustful culture to one that is more supportive of the cultivation of trust requires attention to the underlying assumptions that give rise to behavior. It will require patience and persistence as you challenge these assumptions and help teachers find more productive means to respond to the problems they face in their professional lives.

Key Points About Teachers Trusting One Another

- Principals set the tone for teachers to trust one another.

- Teachers' trust in one another is facilitated by principals who promote a school culture that emphasizes cooperation and caring rather than competition and favoritism.

- In the absence of trust in colleagues' professional competence, teachers may nonetheless trust those teachers as friends or based on their contributions to the overall functioning of the school.

- The effects of betrayal among colleagues can be lasting and can have a detrimental effect on teachers' willingness to be open in sharing teaching strategies, ideas, and resources.

- Schools with a high level of trust among the faculty are more likely to benefit from teacher collaboration and constructive responses to conflict.

- A "can do" attitude is more likely in schools with greater trust among teacher colleagues, resulting in greater effort, persistence, and resilience in the face of difficulties.

- Trust among the teachers in a school makes it more likely that the school will function as a professional learning community.

Questions for Reflection and Discussion

1. What specific actions can you take to foster a greater level of trust among the teachers at your school? What structures can be put in place that will bolster trust?

2. What would it take for you to help your teachers overcome distrust in order to create a culture in which teachers feel free to visit one another's classrooms? How can you foster professional discourse in which teachers discuss teaching methods despite possible disagreements and differences in teaching philosophy? What can you do to foster trust between people with different values or passionately held viewpoints?

3. What kind of teacher induction activities would help new teachers develop a sense of collective trust in each other and in the administrators at your school?

4. How do you maintain a trusting working relationship when you are responsible for collecting documentation on a teacher's mistakes, errors, inconsistencies, and times of procedural error for the good of the organization?

Fostering Trust with Students and Parents

The only way to make a person trustworthy is to trust him.

Henry Lewis Stimson

Trust is fundamental for learning. Consequently, establishing a trusting environment hits schools in their bottom line—student achievement. Principals and teachers need to build trusting relationships with students and parents in order to accomplish their essential goal of fostering student achievement and equipping students for citizenship. When principals, teachers, students, and parents trust each other and work together cooperatively, a climate of success is likely. But when distrust prevails, each is motivated to minimize his or her vulnerability to one another. The result is disengagement from the educational process. Safety comes at the expense of student achievement.

Faculty trust has both a direct and an indirect impact on student achievement. When teachers believe their students are competent and reliable, they create learning environments that facilitate student academic success. A study of trust and achievement demonstrated that the greater the trust in students and parents, the higher the level of school achievement in reading and mathematics, even when the impact of socioeconomic status was held constant (Goddard, Tschannen-Moran, & Hoy, 2001). And in a decade-long study of schools in Chicago that were engaged in a reform initiative, which initially assessed a large number of variables, Bryk and Schneider (2002) came to the conclusion that trust was a critical factor in predicting which schools would make the greatest gains in student achievement and which would sustain those gains over time. In schools where there was a greater level of trust, student achievement was generally higher and the gains were lasting.

Faculty trust also has an indirect influence on student achievement. The level of trust is related to the collective efficacy of the faculty, that is, the extent to which teachers will persist in finding new instructional strategies for students who are failing (Tschannen-Moran & Goddard, 2001; Tschannen-Moran & Barr, 2004). Together, these studies suggest that trust makes schools better places for students to learn by enabling and empowering productive connections between families and schools. Because of the tendency for trust to build on itself, higher student achievement is likely to produce even greater trust, whereas low student achievement could be expected to lead to a self-reinforcing spiral of blame and suspicion on the part of teachers, parents, and students that would further impair student achievement.

Earning Student and Parent Trust

Principals play an important role in creating the context for trust to develop between parents and the school and between teachers and parents. The school leader creates the framework and structure for these relationships and, by example, may set the tone for these interactions as well. Brenda insisted that her teachers make a positive contact with the parent of every student in their classes before they could make calls of a problem-solving nature. She also planned a back-to-school ice cream social each fall for teachers and parents to get to know one another informally. Planning social gatherings, in addition to the more structured back-to-school night, can create opportunities for teachers and parents to engage in trust-building dialogue.

The adage, "They don't care how much you know until they know how much you care," is nowhere more evident than in the relationship of students and parents to schools. Principals and teachers earn the trust of their students first and foremost by demonstrating their care, persuading students and their parents of their underlying good will, even if the process of education at times requires discipline and the correction of misbehavior or misguided thinking. In the classroom, once teachers have demonstrated consistent and firm caring, they have laid the groundwork from which they can push the student to more ambitious learning goals. David, a Brookside teacher, talked about the art of knowing when to push and when to pull a student—the tenuous balance between supporting a student through an ego-threatening hurdle in learning and challenging him or her to higher levels of performance. He explained, "Once I have developed that trust, and they really know I care, then I can push them and learning really takes off." When students trust their teachers, they are more likely to take the risks that new learning entails.

Teaching is more than disseminating information, and much of what inspires children to learn happens in the interpersonal space between student and teacher. The teacher is inviting the student into new ways of seeing and approaching the world, inducting the student into the community of the educated, and into habits of mind that include approaching the world with curiosity, asking for evidence, and not accepting things at face

I WAS CHATTING with a parent about something fun we had done in the classroom and what her daughter had contributed when the mom looked at me and said, "You really like my daughter, don't you?" I said, "Of course I do!" She said, "That's all I need. I need to know she is spending her days with someone who likes her."

Cindy, second grade teacher

value (Meier, 2002). Basic to the transformational processes of school is learning to trust others outside the family, as much of what students learn in school requires them to rely on the written or spoken words of others (Rotter, 1967). Indeed, for students with insecure attachments at home, the opportunity to learn to trust in the context of a caring classroom community can be transformative (Watson, 2003).

Educators need to persuade students and parents not only that they care, but also that they are competent to foster student learning. They should be open in sharing their teaching methods and practices so that parents can become partners in the educational process. Both principals and teachers must also be reliable in following through on the commitments made to students and parents. Finally, school personnel need always to be scrupulously honest in their dealings with families. Withholding important information, telling half-truths, or even outright lies in order to avoid conflict will only damage trust in the long run.

The development of trusting relationships is a critical vehicle not only for improving schools but also in helping to overcome some of the disadvantages of poverty. For teachers to help students access the opportunities that schooling can provide, they need to build trust (Watson, 2003). Without trust, students lose a valuable form of social support. For disadvantaged children whose families lack the cultural capital to prepare their children to access all of the opportunities schools can present, teachers are the primary institutional agents responsible for guiding these students to academic success (Lareau, 1987). Building bridges of trust across social class differences can be a challenge. Statistical analysis of trust relationships within an urban district showed that poverty, more than race or ethnicity, seemed to be the culprit in hindering the trust that would lead to achievement (Tschannen-Moran, 2001). This finding suggests that when teachers draw in-group and out-group distinctions about students, social class is a more potent dividing line than race. Although Brookside, Lincoln, and Fremont all had faculties that were diverse, and some teachers had even started life in disadvantaged circumstances, through education they had largely assumed middle-class values and attitudes that were sometimes at odds with those of the low-income families of their students (Payne, 2001). Schools with high concentrations of poor students are likely to benefit from a focus on the development of trust.

WHEN I ARRIVED, I formed an advisory committee with a representative from each neighborhood. I listened, and listened, and listened, for about four years, at which time the advisory group and the PTA group became one. The PTA group was in too much conflict when I began to have started there.

Peggy, elementary principal

In a study of trust in family-school relationships, parents tended to hold a higher level of trust in teachers than teachers held in parents, and the nature of parent-teacher interactions was a better predictor of trust than was the frequency of the interaction (Adams & Christenson, 2000). This means that teachers can improve the quality of trust relationships simply by improving the tone and helpfulness of their interactions, even if there is no greater frequency. In this study, the income level of families, their ethnicity, and student enrollment in special or regular education had no significant effects on the quality of the family-school trust relationships. Adams and Christenson (2000) proposed that family-school partnerships to enhance students' success are facilitated by goals of the partnership that are centered on improving educational success for students, parents' and teachers' belief in shared responsibility for educational outcomes, two-way communication, nonblaming interactions, and provision of a number of options for meaningful parent participation at the school.

Faculty Trust in Students and Parents

Teachers' trust is key to the relationships that connect students and their families to schools. Teachers' trust is important because teachers are in daily contact with students and are the first line of communication between the school and the family. When teachers and students are committed to academic excellence, teachers trust both parents and students; in turn, when the faculty trusts parents and students, the school is likely to press for high academic achievement. Academic emphasis and faculty's trust in clients are linked; it is difficult to have one without the other (Smith et al., 2001).

When I began my investigation of trust in schools, I looked at trust in students and trust in parents as separate. However, both quantitative and qualitative studies have led to connecting trust in students with trust in parents—faculty's trust in students is inextricably linked to trust in their families. In a statistical analysis of survey data of teachers' responses to questions about their trust in students and their trust in parents, the answers were statistically indistinguishable: when trust in students was high, trust in parents was high; when trust in students was low, trust in parents was low as well. The answers varied together so that trust in students was reflected in trust in parents. Because of the blurring of this distinction, trust in students and trust in parents were merged into a single unit labeled "trust in clients" in the faculty survey provided in the appendices of this book.

Although faculty trust in students was mediated by the recognition that they were children and still learning how to get along in the world, this also led to a blurring of the lines between trust in students and trust in parents. Several teachers said that when a child misbehaved it was not the child they mistrusted but the parents of that child. Christy made this distinction clear: "At this age level I feel that if the child is not trustworthy, it is as a result of the parents. The responsibility isn't really on them at this young age. I tend to get angry with the parents and lose trust with the parents. I don't think I ever lose trust with the child. I get very angry with the parents."

Moreover, David explained that when a child was seen as trustworthy, the trust engendered was extended through the child to the parents: "This just may be a quirk of mine, but I have a great deal of respect for those parents of the students who have earned my trust. Because those qualities are coming from somewhere, and I say those qualities are coming from home. That's what I say."

Benevolence, Reliability, and Respect

Because of the lower position of students in the school hierarchy, the nature of vulnerability between teachers and students was quite different from that among teachers or between teachers and principals, so trust took on a different form. When it came to relationships with students, the dimension of benevolence or good will took on a somewhat narrower definition, most often characterized as respect. In making trust judgments about children, teachers were looking for students with internal control, children who not only exercised self-discipline but who also were willing to cooperate with the system of the school. David explained how the sense that a student was reliable grew from evidence of that self-discipline:

> I am looking for respect. That is what I am looking for. If I see respect, if I see they just behave well, they respect adults, they respect others, they know what school is about in terms of coming, paying attention, not goofing off, not punching or calling names, those are the kids I put my trust in. Those are kids who are usually reliable, dependable. They know what the system is and they are working within the system. They are not rebelling or trying to go against the system. I can count on them, and I can trust them. I can walk out that door and not worry about that child standing up all of a sudden and running across the room and popping somebody or throwing something, or yelling out something inappropriate.

Students and parents who were rude and disrespectful and who blamed others for problems rather than accepting responsibility were more difficult for teachers to trust. Principals are often asked to intervene in situations where teachers are experiencing disrespect from either a student or parent (or both). When principals are able to intervene constructively in these difficult interchanges, it can help initiate a spiral of trust.

Teachers are attuned to whether parents are committed to their children. In making judgments about trust in parents, teachers often mentioned wanting to see a commitment to the child's well-being and to their education. They also were looking for respect extended to them as teachers. David continued:

> I usually trust parents if they are sincere about their child's education. If they come into the building and they don't pose a threat—where they're wanting to look for the negative. When they give you some positive hints or comments, or some positive body language— that makes me feel comfortable. To me that's very important because the better the lines of communication, the better it is for the child. If the child sees that you don't pose a threat to their parents and they don't pose a threat to you, the child fits into that link and then they can feel more confident to come in and share even personal matters.

When teachers felt that parents shared their commitment to the best interests of the child, even if they occasionally disagreed over the means to achieve those ends, they were willing to extend trust to the parents. When confidence that parents had the child's best interests at heart was lacking, teachers were angry and did not feel they had the basis to develop trust with those parents. Rob, a teacher at Lincoln described the challenge he faced with one of his students:

> I have one little girl whose parents, for some reason, play games and don't give her her medication in the morning. But as soon as she takes her pill at 11:00 she is fine.

She is terrible in the morning. She gets so frustrated. She spits, she throws things, she slaps, she gets up, she screams, she leaves the room. At times you get frustrated, but when you think about it, you understand it is not entirely her doing. And then my anger goes to the parents. It has been a long year with this particular family. They don't want to be called at home when the child misbehaves. They want the child identified as disabled, and when the child wasn't identified they got up and stormed out of the room. Personally, I think they wanted money. I think they are using the child. I've heard rumors that they are selling the medication they are supposed to give her in the morning. The child was adopted, and I have my suspicions about why they adopted her.

Teachers also had a sense of what they were owed by parents, and they felt hurt or betrayed when parents did not meet those expectations. Teachers wanted parents to respect their expertise and were bothered when parents questioned their competence, particularly when parents had less education than the teacher. When parents expressed confidence that the teacher cared, teachers in turn found it easier to establish an atmosphere of cooperation and mutual respect. Teachers also wanted parents to deal directly with them when problems arose. Christy described an incident that distressed her in which a parent complained to Brenda about discipline problems in her classroom without discussing the issues with her first.

I did have some trust issues with a couple of my parents at the beginning of the year that I have not forgotten. The first day of school I must have started out wrong because discipline was a real issue for me. It was a very frustrating situation for me as an educator. Really that first month was really hard on me and took a lot out of me. So, one of my parents came in at 2:00 and stayed in our class for the rest of the day. She had always been very supportive of me. She knew the makeup of the class and she admitted that it was a very difficult group. Well, she went to the principal later and said I didn't have good discipline. It really hurt me that to my face she seemed all supportive, and then she went and did that. But it is interesting that as the year has gone on, of course, these parents have changed their whole tune about it. They say, "Oh, my child is reading better than he ever has." But I still remember that because I don't feel it was handled right. I would have preferred if they had come to me instead of going behind my back and talking to the principal.

Christy's anger increased when she learned that the woman's son had had a reputation as a troublemaker in his previous school. Brenda helped by encouraging the parent to deal directly with Christy and by offering to be a part of the conversation if the par-

---

AS A FAMILY, we were very committed to public schools and actively involved in our local school. Then a new principal was assigned to our school who had little administrative training and no experience in an elementary school. That same year our son was assigned a young, inexperienced teacher. Instead of looking for the best in our son, the two of them just saw him as a troublemaker and a problem. He was sent to the principal's office repeatedly. They punished him and shamed him in front of his class. He was isolated, made to sit away from the class, in the hallway, or in other classrooms. Of course, as this went on he became angrier and angrier and acted out more. No one questioned that his behavior might be linked to a learning problem, and they said they could not help it if some of the behavior was brought on because he was bored. It was devastating to watch our charming, clever, if sometimes mischievous, little boy transformed into an angry, hostile, and unhappy child. In the end I felt that I had no choice but to remove him from school and teach him at home.

Zoe, homeschooling mother

ent felt she needed assistance. Christy felt vindicated by the progress she was able to make not only with this boy but with several other troubled students in her class that year.

Honesty

Honesty was a much bigger issue in fostering faculty trust relationships with students than it was with principals and colleagues because this facet of trust was more frequently violated by students. Many of the teachers in this urban context reported that they regularly dealt with problems of students lying or not taking responsibility for their actions. Many, like Rob, reported having students who not only would steal from other students but who also had stolen from teachers: "Most of them I do trust. There's a couple I can't and I don't. A couple of them will go right up and go through the drawers of my desk and take whatever they want. But both of those I am thinking about take medication [for Attention Deficit Disorder]. It's easier knowing it is a medical condition. Maybe if they weren't on medication I would be a little less forgiving."

On the whole, teachers were more forgiving of breaches in honesty from students than they might have been from an adult because they acknowledged that they were just children and that they were still learning.

Openness

Openness on the part of students was not often mentioned as a problem. As Mary commented, "99.9 percent of the children" were willing to talk about themselves if she showed an interest and took the time to listen. She talked about the importance of having time to get to know students in developing a relationship of trust:

> I look for their opening up to me about where their personal life is concerned—what they did at home. Sometimes if a student doesn't share their personal experiences with you, it may be that they are withdrawn

or they may be intimidated by you as an adult. Usually a child just opens up. To me, that's the grounds for trust, because I don't automatically trust a child when they come. I don't think every child is good or not good. It takes time to get to know them. I need background knowledge, and they need background knowledge from me. They need to know they can trust me.

Mary recognized that she could facilitate openness on the part of students and parents not just by showing interest, but also by being willing to share information about her own life.

Early on, it is just my personality to establish rapport with the students and with the parents as soon as I can. Talking to them often, letting them tell their stories. I have a sharing time every day, so they can say what is on their minds and they are not interrupting at other times. If they have a story that relates to my life, then I will share about myself and they just love to hear that. Anytime the parents come in for any reason, I try to take the time to talk with them, try to pull information about their lives, what kinds of jobs they have, what kinds of things they do with their children. When I tell them about myself, then I think they feel more comfortable with me. I

WE HAD A parent who had been very active in fundraising and helping out at the school over a number of years as his children came through. But then it came out that he had been embezzling some of the money he raised. Over all that time, it added up to quite a bit of money. There was a series of articles in the paper about it. I used to feel proud to say where I worked. Now whenever I say the name of our school, that's all people want to talk about. His wrongdoing has overshadowed all of the good things we're doing.

Emma, media specialist

remind them that I have children because then they say, "Oh, you do understand!" I think that really helps.

A willingness to communicate with the teacher enhanced the sense of trust between teachers and parents. When a parent was willing to trust the teacher, it was often reciprocated. When parents discounted what teachers said, narrowly taking their child's side and blaming the teacher or other students for the child's misbehavior, distrust was fostered.

Most teachers wanted to have a partnership with parents, but they acknowledged that they did not often initiate contact with parents unless there was a problem with the student. Brenda insisted that the teachers make a positive contact with every parent in their classroom before they initiated contact of a problem-solving nature. Brenda explored having each classroom wired for a telephone to facilitate communication with parents. When that proved unfeasible, she purchased a portable telephone for each wing. Another program at Brookside aimed to increase the number of positive contacts with parents by sending out postcards to parents when the child had done something well. At Brookside, students were also expected to attend the quarterly conference between home and school. The student led a portion of the conference, which helped the child accept responsibility for his or her learning. The student was the direct recipient of praise for whatever progress had been made but also was the center of the efforts to resolve any difficulties.

Teachers at both Fremont and Lincoln described discipline that was reactive rather than proactive. They described minimal involvement or communication with parents, and what communication existed revolved mostly around problems of student behavior. Brian described his attempts to work with the parent of a student who had started the year as a model student but came back from the winter break a changed child—hostile, unruly, and unkempt. He said the mother had come to the first couple of conferences to address this problem but then stopped coming or even returning phone calls. There were very few social encounters between teachers and parents. Even when events were planned, attendance was minimal.

When there was a high level of trust in parents and students, there was more likely to be a high level of collaboration between parents and the faculty. When students could be counted on to respect the systems and structures of school, and when parents could be trusted to engage constructively with teachers, a climate of openness in decision making was also evident. When there was greater trust in parents, there was less defensiveness on the part of the principal and the faculty and a greater willingness to share authority. With a greater sense of shared purpose, there was more room at the decision-making table (Hoy & Tschannen-Moran, 1999; Tschannen-Moran, 2001).

Competence

Competence in students had more to do with their conduct as students, a willingness to go along with the structures of school, than with academic competence. In making trust judgments about parents, competence in basic parenting skills was important. When teachers felt their jobs were made more difficult because of the lack

---

A MOTHER OF two middle-school students moved into our area. She announced to me that she was not going to send her children to the neighborhood school. I explained that she had a legal obligation to make sure her children were educated, and her only other option was to teach her children at home. The woman declared that that was what she wanted to do. But when she read over the documents I requested from the state on what would be required, she had to admit that she was not prepared to homeschool her children. When I probed further about her resistance to sending her children to school, she declared, "I don't trust the principal." Puzzled, I asked, "You just moved here, how can you know that you don't trust the principal?" The woman replied angrily, "I know because he was my principal when I was in junior high!"

Robert, social worker

I HAD A little boy last year that came from a poor, dysfunctional family. He was the oldest of five children and everybody had different fathers. They did a lot of moving. I think he could have learned easily if he had been in a stable environment and had the emotional support. He was very hyperactive, always trying to threaten the other children, hurting them when he got the chance. No respect for other children, not even respect for adults. Although I would get angry at him for his behaviors, I was so mad at the mother. I put all my frustration at the parents. There was nothing else wrong with him other than that he never had the consistency of a normal family. It was so frustrating.

Barbara, second grade teacher

of competence of parents to provide basic necessities and structure for their children, trust in parents was more difficult to establish. Teachers recognized that some parents were at a loss as to how to discipline or care for their child. David recognized the complexity of parenting and was willing to give most parents the benefit of the doubt: "Some are to the point that they don't know what else to do. They say, 'I tried this, I tried that.' I'm sure in their own way they will do what they can."

Schools can assist overwhelmed parents in finding constructive ways to care for and discipline their children. When families fail to respond in kind, they need to be confronted with kindness and understanding rather than judgment and disdain in order to foster norms that support mutual respect and trustworthiness.

Most of the teachers felt a genuine fondness and caring for their students, even if they were sometimes frustrated by the amount of time and energy they had to devote to disciplining them. In establishing trust relationships with students, above all they were looking for respect and reliability. For many there was more leeway in their definition of trust with students because the expectation they had for them as children was different from what they expected from other adults or colleagues. In developing trust with parents, teachers above all wanted to see that there was a commitment to the child's well-being and education. When teachers invested themselves in their students, they wanted to feel that caring was acknowledged and shared by parents. They wanted to feel there was a unity of purpose.

Putting It into Action

As principal, you set the tone for trusting relationships with students and parents through the example you set. If you are heard complaining about your interactions with students and parents or speaking about them in disrespectful ways, it will send the message to other adults in the building that that is an appropriate way to think and feel. It may also communicate frustration, giving the impression that you doubt your ability to bring about productive change and do not know what else to do. You can help foster trusting relationships among teachers, students, and their families by creating structures for teachers to make positive connections with parents and opportunities for productive engagement and problem solving.

You have the opportunity to demonstrate both your caring and your competence as you engage in proactive strategies to support students into achieving success. Your focus should be on success in both academic performance and behavior. This may involve a reassessment of the schoolwide discipline policy and practices, as well as mechanisms for intervening when students begin to fall behind. Earning a reputation for consistency and fairness will pay dividends as you are involved in discipline and exercise your responsibility to shape the character of the young people in your care.

Within the bounds of good judgment, engaging in humor and play will show your trust of students and your willingness to be vulnerable with them. This behavior should never involve humor that is demeaning, sarcastic, or inappropriate but can be a means of building bonds of trust that makes the school a place where people want to be.

Key Points About Fostering Trust with Students and Parents

- For teachers, the lines between trusting students and trusting parents are blurred. If teachers can't trust the students, they tend not to trust the parent.

- Teachers want to feel that their professional competence is respected and their caring for their students acknowledged.

- Bridges of trust can be more difficult for teachers to build with low-income families because teachers are less confident that they share the same cultural values and ethical standards.

- Efforts on the part of teachers and principals to foster more open and frequent communication with parents and more opportunities for parents to be involved in decisions resulted in greater trust.

- Principals can help set the tone for trusting relationships with students and parents by engaging in proactive strategies to make positive connections with parents and support students into achieving success.

Questions for Reflection and Discussion

1. What actions could you take to help foster more productive and trusting relationships between students and teachers in your school?

2. What activities does your school use to engage parents? How are parents made to feel welcomed as valued partners in the educational process? What supports are offered to parents who are struggling with the challenging and complex task of raising their children?

3. What specific strategies could you employ to assure students, parents, and members of the community that you care and are trustworthy?

8

Restoring Trust

Hold a tight rein over the three T's—thought,
temper and tongue—and you will have few regrets.

Anonymous

There is both good news and bad news when it comes to repairing broken trust. The good news is that in many instances,
damaged trust can be repaired. The bad news is that the restoration
of trust is an arduous process that requires humility and effort and
may extend over a long period. What is required to repair trust will
depend on what caused the disruption of trust in the first place.
Whether distrust has grown from hurt pride over a perceived insult,
disillusionment that grows out of broken rules or norms, or the
recognition of real differences in basic values, attention will need
to be paid to these issues in the restoration of trust. If you judge that
a person you are engaged with in some endeavor of mutual interest
is irresponsible or untrustworthy, that assessment should be the
beginning of a conversation—the beginning of a transformation
from distrust to trust (Solomon & Flores, 2001). Such conversations
are by no means easy or comfortable. But the willingness to engage
in a constructive, albeit difficult, conversation is a concrete and
powerful way to show that you care.

In rebuilding trust, it is important to recognize the distinction
between disappointment and betrayal. Failures and resulting

disappointments are an inevitable part of human relationships because human beings are imperfect. Betrayal is an intentional act that has resulted in possible or actual harm to the victim. Solomon and Flores (2001) warn that "to confuse failure with betrayal is to set yourself up for no creativity, no innovation, no adventure, no intimacy, no trust, no life at all" (p. 130). If trust is diminished due to a lack of reliability or because a person's competence proves inadequate for the task at hand, it may or may not constitute a betrayal. A betrayal implies a lack of sufficient caring combined with dishonesty.

Repairing Broken Trust

Principals often find themselves between a rock and a hard place, seemingly having to play the needs of one constituent off those of another. It can feel like there is no course of action that will not damage the trust of one group or another. This was the situation that Brenda found herself in when salary negotiations reached an impasse in Brookside's district. The union called for the teachers to "work-to-rule," meaning that they would fulfill contractual obligations to the letter but not by a minute more. This is one of the union's most powerful tactics, because schools rely on teachers to go far beyond minimal obligations in order to run effective and productive schools. Kathy explained the tough spot that both Brenda and the teachers were in as a result:

> With the "work-to-rule" at the beginning of this school year, we weren't suppose to stay for any after school meetings. But then we had a huge debate about Grade Level Night because that's the night when parents get to talk to their child's teacher about what's going to happen in the classroom. Brenda felt very strongly about having it, so we gave in because we understood her reasons. She came to us with a very pleading heart. She told us that

she wouldn't force us to do things but just to talk about
it. We said we understood where she was coming from, so
we gave in. I don't know if we should have, but we did.

The hard feelings from that time put a strain on Brenda's relationship with her teachers. Some felt that they should not have
been put in the position of having to choose between loyalty to the
union and loyalty to Brenda and the school. Those teachers felt it
was a betrayal of the care they had come to expect from Brenda.
More than six months later, the effects were still being felt in the
relationship. Kathy continued: "Just last week somebody said
'Regardless of all she does for us, she is still an administrator.' As
much as she values us and will make concessions for what we need,
she still has to run her building. It's hard. That's the only time I
really felt bad here." Brenda was put in a position of having to repair
damaged trust and mend the relationship with her teachers.

Repairing trust is a two-way process in which each side must perceive that the short- or long-term benefits to be gained from the
relationship are sufficiently valued to be worth the investment of
time and energy required by the repair process. Each party must
decide that the benefits of restoring the relationship are preferable
to finding other ways to meet the needs that once were met by the
relationship (Lewicki & Bunker, 1996). The violator and the victim have different roles and responsibilities in the reestablishment
of trust. The process of repair often is initiated by the victim, who
verbally or nonverbally confronts the violator and makes him or her
aware of the sense of betrayal. But it can also be initiated by the perpetrator, who feels contrite and wants to make things right again
in the relationship. Regardless of how the repair process is initiated,
the violator then has the opportunity to engage in the "four A's
of absolution": admit it, apologize, ask forgiveness, and amend your
ways. The teachers who felt it had been inappropriate for Brenda
to ask the teachers to go forward with the Grade Level Night
as planned, rather than to reschedule after the labor dispute was

settled, found various ways, both subtle and not so subtle, to let Brenda know that they were harboring bad feelings. Finally, Brenda raised the issue at a faculty meeting to clear the air.

Admit It

To begin with, the violator must acknowledge that a violation has occurred and that harm was done. Listening carefully to the victim is a sign of respect and signals a willingness to engage in a process of rebuilding the relationship. To dismiss the harm as insignificant is disrespectful to the experience of the victim and the risk the victim may have experienced in arranging the confrontation. Brenda opened the topic for discussion, noting the changes in attitude and behavior that she had witnessed that made her suspect there were unresolved feelings. She listened to the teachers share what a difficult position her desire to go forward with Grade Level Night had placed them in, when all the other schools in the district had canceled theirs. Whereas teachers reported that were normally proud to say they taught at Brookside, they said that they had taken flak during that time from teachers in other buildings, as well as from the union, for breaking ranks.

The perpetrator must accept responsibility for the effects of his or her actions. The violator must admit to having caused the event and also admit that it was destructive. Even if the harm was unintentional, the violator needs to acknowledge that the way events unfolded and in the experience of the victim, harm was done. People who immediately make excuses and who shift blame to someone or something else provoke wariness and frustration rather than signaling a willingness to reestablish a trusting relationship. The energy they spend in self-protection would be better spent facing up to the damage they have done and looking for solutions. The need to absolve oneself from legitimate guilt will interfere with rebuilding trust. Although Brenda was stung by the accusation that her desire to go forward with Grade Level Night on the scheduled date was motivated as much by the desire to enhance her own reputation as to start the year with good communication with the parents as she said, she avoided becoming outwardly defensive or lashing out at those calling into question her commitment to the school. Nor did she remind the teachers that she had left the final decision to them. Instead she accepted responsibility for the way her request had forced teachers to make a painful choice in a situation in which they felt divided loyalties.

Apologize

To apologize is to not only admit that harm was done and that one's actions contributed to that harm but also to express regret for one's behavior. Trust is enhanced by a willingness to apologize for the unpleasant consequences of one's actions (Greenberg, 1993; Konovsky & Pugh, 1994). Solomon and Flores (2001) remind us that, "an apology is a statement of an intention to redeem oneself, and the beginning of a conversation about how this can be done" (p. 133). Brenda apologized for how the request and the decision to go forward with Grade Level Night had not only caused dissention and hurt feelings within the school but had also resulted in their pride in being Brookside teachers to be, at least temporarily, a cause for derision among their colleagues across the district. Because the labor dispute had not been protracted and had, in fact, been settled not long after the disputed event, Brenda admitted that the Grade Level Night could have been rescheduled without undue loss to parent-school communications.

An apology can, in some cases, be sufficient to restore the relationship because in admitting wrong there is an implicit understanding that one will endeavor to avoid repeating the error in the future. But the perpetrator should not assume that the apology erases the error for which it has been issued. To rush too readily to the conclusion that all is now well violates the sense of care that undergirds the trusting relationship and the sense that one will take the needs and desires of the other seriously. It is often necessary for the perpetrator to ask for forgiveness and to demonstrate a willingness to make amends for his or her errors.

Ask Forgiveness

If trust is to be repaired, some form of forgiveness is required. Forgiveness can be transformative, but it may not be easy to achieve. Forgiveness is a process in which the victim reaches out to the betrayer and expresses a willingness to become vulnerable once again. Forgiveness is not simply a state of mind; it is an action—or a sequence of actions—and a ritualized undoing of the act of betrayal. Forgiveness can be facilitated when the perpetrator makes an explicit request to be forgiven. Solomon and Flores (2001) discuss the importance of spoken statements in the process of forgiveness:

> Forgiveness does not always have to be verbally articulated and formally expressed in the public realm, but in practice, this is what happens. One can indicate that one has forgiven a betrayal, for instance, by simply acting toward the betrayer as if there is nothing wrong, although this carries with it the liability that such behavior may well be interpreted as mere artifice, to trick the betrayer into lowering his or her defenses before getting even in some equally hurtful way. Or the absence of explicit forgiveness may indicate that the person betrayed simply does not take this particular betrayal—or the betrayer—seriously, which may constitute an offense in its own right. For such reasons, an explicit verbal act, paradigmatically some form of "I forgive you" or "Forget it" is particularly desirable (p. 140).

Forgiveness may restore trust, but it will probably not return the relationship to its former state. Even if the victim is willing to extend forgiveness in order to restore the relationship, it is unlikely that he or she will forget. Victims can often recall vivid details about a significant betrayal at work even decades afterward (Jones & Burdette, 1994). But if the betrayal is placed firmly in the past, and overcome (but not erased) by forgiveness, the commitment to the relationship on both sides may be strengthened so that greater care and attention is paid to the relationship and trust is deepened (Solomon & Flores, 2001).

Amend Your Ways

It is the victim who determines what is required to restore trust. This often entails specifying acts of reparation designed to demonstrate that the violator is sincere and committed in the desire to rebuild the relationship, and to demonstrate a willingness to incur a certain amount of personal loss in doing so. The acts of reparation set by the victim may seem in the eyes of the perpetrator to be either reasonable or unreasonable, resulting in either a willingness or unwillingness to meet them. If undertaken, the victim then has the opportunity to judge the sincerity and commitment of the violator as he or she carries out these actions. Reparation also creates an opportunity for the violator to work out any guilt that he or she may have over the harm that was done, whether it was intentional or unintentional (Lewicki & Bunker, 1996).

It may be that the victim refuses to accept any actions, terms, or conditions for reestablishing the relationship. The damage done may be perceived to be so extensive that the victim is no longer willing to continue the relationship and risk being subjected to the possibility of further harm. Or it may be that the victim has sufficient alternatives to get his or her needs met elsewhere to make the effort required in rebuilding trust too arduous. Should the victim refuse to extend forgiveness under any circumstances, continuing in an interdependent relationship is likely to be fraught with tension, poor communication, and lower productivity.

Another fall tradition at Brookside was the annual Camp Night, when the students stayed at the school on a Friday afternoon for an activity and then an overnight sleepover. Each teacher, including resource teachers, had a group of students of mixed-grade levels and engaged in hands-on, fun learning activities. The parents joined in the fun, and the PTA provided a meal. At the end of the evening there was a program, and then everyone slept at the school. Although the event was a lot of work, it was an important community-building event for the school. It was also very important to Brenda. The teachers especially complained about sleeping at school, so in light of teachers' having stepped up for Grade Level Night, and as a way to make amends, Brenda conceded the sleepover aspect of Camp Night that fall.

Although the conflict over Grade Level Night had accentuated the differences in role responsibilities between Brenda and her teachers, it had also caused a reassessment of how much both sides valued the normally cooperative relations and in many ways strengthened the resolve on both sides to care for the quality of that relationship in the future. Brenda's handling of the situation in a forthright and open way made her a role model for the teachers in their own disputes with one another. Putting a betrayal behind but not out of mind, and moving on through the public act of forgiving, can bring healing even after a very painful episode.

Factors That Facilitate Restoring Trust

Trust is fundamental to cooperation, and yet trust can be difficult to establish once a cycle of suspicion, competition, and retaliation has begun. Even in the midst of tension and conflict, trust can be fostered through the conciliatory initiatives of one party acting unilaterally by signaling the desire to establish trust without sacrificing the genuine need to protect his or her interests (Fisher & Brown, 1988). Trust repair is facilitated by working for good communication, being meticulously reliable, and using persuasion rather than coercion. It is also facilitated by constructive attitudes, clear boundaries, communication of promises and credible threats, and constructive conflict resolution strategies.

Unconditionally Constructive Attitudes and Actions

Although relationships necessarily have two parties, it takes only one of these parties to change the quality of the relationship. Even in situations of mutual suspicion, each side has the opportunity for improving the level of trust in the relationship. Each person has the opportunity to adopt "unconditionally constructive attitudes and actions" (Fisher & Brown, 1988). These include trying to understand the other side's interests, attitudes, and beliefs and taking an attitude of acceptance toward the other side. There are many contexts in which we have to interact with individuals and groups of whose conduct we do not approve. We can work to understand even if we do not condone their behavior or become convinced of the correctness of their point of view. In trying to understand the other party and their motivations, one should assume that others do not see themselves as bad people pursuing immoral ends through illegitimate means but that they have what they consider good reasons for doing as they do. Their justification may grow out of a value system that

---

I TOOK OVER a school that was filled with conflict and total lack of trust. It was divided between those who were loyal to the previous principal and those who opposed him. That first year, I had mugs printed with the slogan "Children are not things to be molded but gifts to be unfolded." I wanted to put the emphasis on the children as a way to create some common ground. I began a tradition of hosting a barbeque at my house four times a year. That was neutral ground. Had we had it at the home of a teacher from one faction or the other, some teachers would not have come. Those turned out to be important occasions where teachers met family members and got to know each other away from the building. Teachers shared with me how much they appreciated those events and the emphasis on students.

Peggy, elementary principal

differs from your own, but it can help create a context for conversation about their rationale for the behavior you find offensive.

Communication of Clear Boundaries

Feelings of violation can result in a sense of betrayal. We assume that others understand how we want to be treated, but this is not always clear. People differ according to their personality, as well as cultural norms and understandings about what is acceptable. It is important in creating a context for trusting relationships to set clear boundaries about how one expects to be treated. There are four stages or levels in the establishment of clear boundaries, escalating from *inform* to *request* to *demand* to, finally, if necessary, *leave* (Coach U, 2003).

The first stage is to inform the other party about how you want to be treated, and perhaps about how their current behavior violates those desires. Too often, people assume that others know or will figure out what they want through the interpretation of nonverbal cues and signs of irritation, hoping to spare themselves the effort and discomfort of having to articulate their needs. But this strategy leaves open the possibility that the other party simply will not "get it." They may have a different set of understandings about how people are to be treated, based on different cultural backgrounds or personality. For example, a person from New York City may hold assumptions altogether different from those of a person raised in the rural South as to what is considered to be polite or acceptable ways of interacting with one another. Each may misinterpret or be at a loss as to what is meant by nonverbal cues sent by the other.

The second phase is to make an explicit request as to the behavior that is desired. Ideally, this is communicated in a firm, even tone before irritation has come to characterize this aspect of the relationship. A common mistake that people make is to skip over the first two steps, letting anger build with each breach until they reach the third stage, to demand, thus making it a starting point instead of a late stage in a process. They count each violation as a betrayal, based on the assumption that there has been a mutual understanding of common principles, when this, in fact, may not be the case. The final phase, if continual efforts have not created a situation in which one's boundaries are respected, is to leave. It may be inconvenient and disruptive to leave a relationship and have to figure out how else to have those needs met, and it may mean giving up on a cherished joint project. But if the level of violation is serious enough, leaving may be worth all that it costs.

Firm Promises and Credible Threats

In situations in which we are attempting to build or restore trust, it is important to be very mindful of the words we use, as language is the primary vehicle needed to establish trust. Such care is especially important when making either promises or threats. Neither should be spoken unless one has every intention of following through. If some unforeseen set of circumstances prevents the fulfillment of a promise, the promisor owes an explanation and an apology to the one that was promised. To overcome distrust, one party announces a clear, conciliatory initiative—a promise grounded in good will

---

I WORKED WITH a man from the Middle East who was very aggressive and it seemed to me very judgmental. It seemed like he had to challenge everything I said. The relationship finally reached a breaking point, when I told him how hurt and angry I was feeling all of the time. I told him the negative impact it was having on my enjoyment of my work life, to the point where I was ready to put in for a transfer. He was surprised to learn I was so unhappy. He explained, "Where I come from, everything's an argument. There isn't anything in my culture that is not an argument. It's the way we express affection, acceptance, prices, news—you know? Everything." He had never before told me that, or invited me into that knowledge of his culture. After that conversation, he was able to tone down his argumentativeness with me, and I was able to be less sensitive to his remarks so we could work much better together.

Janine, high school special education teacher

toward the other with the intention of aiding in the mutual project that is the basis of the interdependence. It is then crucial to carry out this promise reliably. This gesture is then followed by an explicit invitation (but not a demand) for the other party to reciprocate.

Making credible threats can be as important to building trust as keeping promises. In any ongoing system, violations are likely to occur, if only by chance, but the system of interchange will break down if violations are frequent and go unchecked, as they did at Fremont. Each person must have a way of reacting to violations, a credible threat, which is known to the other and can serve to inhibit violations. The perception that another person is powerless and either unable or unwilling to retaliate for inappropriate behavior can invite exploitation. Even one example of the willingness to retaliate for broken trust, however, can help support trust. At Fremont, Fred's continual threats that he "was not going to tolerate" certain behavior, in the absence of any action year after year, caused him to lose credibility. His unwillingness to follow through on threats led to a lack of trust.

When holding people accountable, however, it is important that it be done discretely and in a way that preserves the persons' dignity. Gloria's willingness to publicly humiliate teachers who had challenged her authority or to make an example of poorly performing teachers by treating them badly in front of the faculty was seen as a betrayal of the rules of fair play within the school. It cost her the trust of her teachers. In rebuilding trust, the golden rule of treating others as you would want to be treated is a good guide to behavior, especially in a time of conflict. Going a step further and honoring how *they* want to be treated is even better.

Establishing good communication is key to reestablishing trust. Trust is much harder to establish in the absence of communication. Without honest communication, once suspicion has come to characterize a relationship and an escalating cycle of retaliation and revenge has set in, it is extremely difficult to reestablish trust. The use of promises is important in building a mutually cooperative strategy.

Protection Without Escalation

Blind trust, or trust that is extended beyond what is reasonable given the information available about the others' actions and motivations, is dangerous and does not rebuild trust. However, each party does have the opportunity to be completely trustworthy. When one suspects another of harboring negative intentions, then one must take defensive action to protect one's interests. However, these actions can reinforce the suspicions of the other party that one means to do him or her harm. Thus, an escalating cycle of distrust and competition ensues. Breaking that cycle involves protecting one's interests while signaling to the other the desire to negotiate a mutually beneficial relationship.

Expecting exact reciprocity in relationships can be problematic because such expectations risk disillusionment or even escalation of the conflict (Fisher & Brown, 1988). A tit-for-tat strategy does not work in most situations because in real-life relationships, the meaning of a particular action, whether one of cooperation or defection, is not always clear and may be an issue of dispute. An exact reciprocation may be hard to gauge because victims and perpetrators often use "different arithmetics" in assessing the harm done to them as opposed to that inflicted on the opponent.

Conflict Resolution

Without trust, negotiating a bilateral agreement to reverse an escalating cycle of betrayal and revenge can be quite difficult. Conflict resolution is a process of problem solving designed to negotiate a solution that each party can live with. When setting up a conflict resolution session, the first decision will involve finding a time and a space conducive to the conversation that needs to take place, where both sides will feel comfortable and interruptions can be minimized. There are various ways that the parties in a dispute can signal a cooperative attitude as a prelude to the conflict resolution meeting. One such cue is to address the person by their proper name or how they like to be addressed as a sign of respect. In some cultures, making eye contact is a sign of openness, although in other cultures it may be interpreted as aggressiveness or disrespect, especially if the parties are of different social standing.

The conflict resolution session begins with an agreement to abide by certain ground rules. These include a commitment to speak truthfully and respectfully, and not to interrupt but to wait for one's turn to speak. The first to present his or her side may be the person who initiated the meeting, the one who is most visibly upset, or the one with the lower position or status if there is a difference. Addressing the other disputant directly, the speaker reveals how he or she is feeling and the behavior of the other that caused those feelings. It is important that the speaker use "I messages" to reveal information about his or her own reactions rather than asserting information about the other ("you messages"). People often resent being told what they thought, felt, or intended by someone else. Each person gets to be the expert on themselves. A "you message" assertion is likely to lead the other person to become defensive, and consequently to be less willing to engage productively in the process or extend himself or herself for the other. Revealing one's hurt and pain, without aggression or blame, can create a context that is more conducive to the other person's responsiveness. This is followed by an explicit request as to what is needed to restore the relationship.

When the first person has finished sharing, the second reflects back, or restates, what he or she has heard, being careful to be both accurate and thorough. The second party then reveals his or her own feelings about the situation and makes a request as to what is needed to restore the relationship. The first party reciprocates by reflecting back what he or she has heard from the other about his or her feelings and needs. Then both parties engage in problem

WE HAVE A strong emphasis on conflict resolution skills at our school. Our school is in an urban neighborhood known for violence, so we are very committed to giving our students the skills for resolving differences peacefully. The returning teachers are always the ones to train new teachers in the process we use. We let them know it isn't just for the kids—we expect them to use the same process for the difficulties we have with each other too. Once they learn it, they get all excited and come back and tell how it has worked with other people in their lives outside of school!

Anne, fourth grade teacher

solving, offering solutions that they perceive will meet the needs of both parties. If after considerable effort a solution that is fully satisfactory to both sides has not been found, compromise alternatives that at least partially meet the needs of each side may be considered. When an acceptable solution is agreed upon, both sides make an explicit commitment to abide by the agreement.

Repairing trust can be a difficult and time-consuming process. However, by adopting constructive attitudes, establishing good boundaries, clearly communicating promises and reliably fulfilling them, and engaging in conflict resolution strategies, trust can once again come to characterize the relationship.

A Context for Repairing Trust

Schools are social systems and, as such, the interpersonal relationships in them are embedded in a social context. That social context not only reflects but shapes the trust relationships in it. The social context and the gossip that takes place in an organization have the effect of pushing trust relationships to extremes—enhancing high trust and driving low trust even lower (Burt & Knez, 1996). In a trusting environment, the benefit of doubt is extended and trust is reinforced, whereas in an atmosphere of distrust a similar set of actions can serve to diminish a weak level of trust even further.

Examples of broken trust were not limited to the low-trust schools. Almost all of the teachers interviewed could give an example of when their trust had been broken either by the principal or by a colleague. The difference was that in the high-trust schools, the rift had eventually been repaired, whereas in low-trust schools resentment had festered, sometimes over long periods. In a trusting context, there was greater likelihood that people would take the risk of repairing trust because they were supported by greater hopefulness of a positive outcome. People gave one another the benefit of the doubt. In the low-trust schools, there were fewer reports of attempts to repair damaged trust. The wounds were still tender. Feuds were carried on from year to year. Ongoing distrust was a drain on the energy, imagination, and vitality of both Lincoln and Fremont schools. The faculty was less able to respond to the needs of students. These schools were not places where people looked forward to coming to work each day. In these schools, a self-perpetuating cycle of distrust seemed to drive trust even lower. Once distrust has taken hold, a spiral of distrust sets in such that even innocent or neutral comments or actions are often read with suspicion (Govier, 1992).

Although Brenda was highly respected at Brookside, she had the reputation of occasionally being short-tempered with members of her staff. People were willing to overlook this shortcoming and forgive her because of her overall dedication and level of support for them. Kathy described how Brenda's caring created the context for forgiveness:

> I think people are willing to go to bat for her because she will go to bat for them. When she may not be having a good day and it just seems that she is upset with you personally, people are willing to step back and say, "This is not how she operates. This is not the norm." I am willing to step up and give her the benefit of the doubt that there is something external to me. I have even heard when she has responded negatively, the person was able

to go back to her and tell her that they didn't think it was right. She apologized, admitted her mistake, and everything was fine. We all coach each other and with the new teachers we tell them, "Don't worry, that's just the way she does sometimes. She'll be fine. She is not out to get you." There is that support there to help that person understand.

Brookside teachers were willing to extend forbearance when Brenda was having a bad day and was unnecessarily short-tempered with a teacher. The story that circulated of Brenda's willingness to apologize when confronted by a teacher built trust even among teachers who had not been the recipient of such an apology themselves. As a consequence of the trust invested in this principal, new faculty members were coached not to take these outbursts personally and to let them go. This example illustrates how a cycle of trust builds even greater trust, and the involvement of third parties can strengthen the trust in a high-trust environment (Burt & Knez, 1996). Incidents that might be interpreted as a breach of trust are neutralized by the overall sense of trust.

At Brookside, it was more likely that when trust was damaged it would be repaired. Teachers were more willing to talk with the person who had violated their trust, even when their usual tendency would be to not say anything and just avoid that person. Because they had an interest in maintaining the positive working environment and because they could anticipate a caring response, they were willing to risk sharing their feelings with the person who had offended them. Once aired, these grievances could be dealt with and trust restored. Kathy described a situation in which her feelings had been hurt, and she let her colleagues know what was bothering her with the expectation that her feelings would be taken seriously:

There was one time this year where two of the other fifth grade teachers started rotating students for certain subjects with each other and I felt kind of excluded, I guess. Once my feelings were known, we talked about it and got everybody's feelings out in the open. It wasn't done intentionally at all. They told me that they had done it on a whim because they needed to do something at that time. And then they were supposedly trying it out to see if it would work among the whole fifth grade. They are very good friends outside of school, so I think they were just talking and just did it. They didn't realize that it had hurt me. When I told them how much it did, we talked about it and debriefed everything. We understood each other's point of view and went on.

With an explanation and an apology, Kathy was willing to accept that the action had not been done maliciously, so she was able to let her hurt feelings go and move on.

In trusting school environments, there was also a greater willingness to give the students the benefit of doubt. There was a greater recognition that the students were, after all, just children and could be expected to make some mistakes in judgment. There seemed to be more of a tendency to be lenient with students, at least on the first or second offense, and to give them the opportunity to rebuild the trust that had been lost. In the high-trust schools, teachers had more positive contacts with parents. These were opportunities to build trust with the parents, creating relational resources that could be "spent" in addressing the inevitable problems that arose. The high level of trust throughout the school community created the context in which breeches of trust would be resolved and greater trust fostered.

Putting It into Action

Trust is a critical resource for schools. It is unlikely that the mission of your school can be accomplished without it. When trust has been disrupted, and when conflicts have resulted in feelings of betrayal, it is important for mechanisms to be in place to help members of the school community restore their broken relationships. As the leader of the school, it is your responsibility to make sure that these mechanisms are in place so that the distrust resulting from unresolved disputes does not impair the ability of your school community to fulfill mutual goals. Because of the arduous and uncertain nature of trust repair, you are far better off avoiding broken trust whenever possible.

Conflict is an inevitable part of the change process. Even where there is agreement on the goals of the change, there will be differences of opinion as to how to achieve those goals. Change disrupts the power dynamics within a school, advantaging some and disadvantaging others. And change involves loss. It disrupts the way people make meaning of their lives at work. As people in your school cope with the loss inherent in change, it is important for you to recognize their reactions as normal grief responses and not to take them personally. Their reaction need not be interpreted as evidence that the change is the wrong direction to go, or that those resisting are bad people if they are less than enthusiastic at the prospect of doing things differently. Listening skillfully and well to people as they react to change can help them move through their grief reactions and can be a powerful way to build trust in the midst of change.

Key Points About Restoring Trust

- To restore trust, each side must believe that the effort is worth it when weighed against having their needs met another way.

- The violator and the victim have different roles and responsibilities in the reestablishment of trust. The principal can be a powerful role model in how to restore trust.

- The four A's of absolution are admit it, apologize, ask forgiveness, and amend your ways.

- The four stages of setting boundaries escalate from inform to request to demand and then, if necessary, to leave.

- Trust repair is bolstered by unconditionally constructive attitudes and actions, communication of boundaries, conciliatory promises and credible threats, as well as conflict resolution strategies.

Questions for Reflection and Discussion

1. Recall a time when a relationship you've been involved in has been restored after a betrayal. Did the process include the four A's of Absolution?

2. Consider an incident that led you to forgive but not forget. What contributed to the restoration? Was the relationship stronger or weaker after the betrayal?

3. When have you been aware of "different arithmetics" at work as a conflict escalated?

4. How have you set clear boundaries with the members of your school community? Did you inform and request before you reached a point of needing to demand? Under what circumstances would you feel like you needed to leave?

5. What could you as a school leader do to intervene in a long-standing feud between two teachers or groups of teachers in a school to help them rebuild trust with one another for the good of the school?

9

Becoming a Trustworthy Leader

*To be trusted is a greater compliment than to be
loved.*

George MacDonald

Throughout this book we have seen how the five facets
of trust—benevolence, honesty, openness, reliability, and
competence—relate to the five constituencies of schools (administrators, teachers, students, parents, and the general public). These
considerations have demonstrated the importance of trust to building successful schools. We have also seen how the absence of trust
impedes effectiveness and progress. If trust breaks down among any
constituency, it can spread like a cancer by eroding academic performance and ultimately undermining the tenure of the instructional leader. In this day and age, no leader can long survive the
demise of trust.

School leaders need to build trust with teachers because
although governance structures such as collaborative decision making and site-based management can bring the insights of more people to solving the complex problems of schooling, they depend upon
trust (Hoy & Tarter, 2003; Smylie & Hart, 1999). Without trust,
communication becomes constrained and distorted, thus making
problems more difficult to resolve (Roberts & O'Reilly, 1974). A

proliferation of rules stemming from a lack of trust causes resentment and alienation among teachers and students alike (Fox, 1974; Govier, 1992). Even when school leaders work to build a common vision and foster acceptance of group goals, without trust these leaders do not inspire their constituencies to go beyond minimum requirements (Podsakoff et al., 1990; Tschannen-Moran, 2003).

Teachers need trust to cope with the stress of changing expectations and the demands of accountability being asked of them. As teachers are asked to change their fundamental beliefs and instructional techniques, they need to build new professional communities anchored in trust and teamwork (Little, 1990; Putnam & Borko, 1997). Even within the classroom, relationships are shifting to forms that require greater trust. Cooperative learning and project-based learning create higher levels of interdependence, which demand higher levels of trust.

Students need trust to engage productively with the learning environment at school and to access the opportunities made available to them (Meier, 2002). Without trust, students' energies are diverted toward self-protection and away from the learning process. Learning to trust the people at school can be a transformative experience for students whose lives outside of school have not taught them to trust (Watson, 2003).

Schools need the trust of parents and the wider school community. Making parents more active partners in the educational process involves fostering trusting relationships. Including parents in school governance requires trust that they will be motivated to work for the common good, not just their own narrow interests. Garnering additional resources from the community through entrepreneurial efforts and partnerships requires trust that the school is making the most of the resources it already has. In short, school leaders need to foster trust within each of the constituencies of their schools.

At the same time that schools face a greater need for trust, they encounter many obstacles to fostering trust. The difficulties of achieving new and higher societal expectations for equity in schools have led to suspicion of schools and school personnel. Higher standards and greater accountability have fostered conditions of distrust and blame. Moreover, schools have to cope with greater diversity and transience. A multicultural society with diverse values and shifting populations makes the cultivation of trust a significant challenge. Adding to this formidable task is the tendency for distrust, once established, to be self-perpetuating. There is a propensity for news of broken trust to spread faster and further than news of intact or restored trust, and the media often feed off of and aggravate the spiral of distrust.

For schools to realize the kinds of positive transformation envisioned by school reform efforts, attention must be paid to issues of trust. Finding ways to overcome the breakdown of trust is essential if we want schools to reach the aspirations we hold for them. This challenge is one of the most important tasks facing school leaders at the start of the twenty-first century.

Trustworthy School Leadership

The principal sets the tone for a school. The principal's behavior has a significant influence on the culture of the school. If schools are to reap the rewards of a trusting work environment, it is the principal's responsibility to build and sustain trusting relationships (Whitener et al., 1998). In order to understand how this works in practical terms, it is useful to consider the five facets of trust in relation not only to the five constituencies of schools but also in relation to the five functions of instructional leaders. These functions include visioning, modeling, coaching, managing, and mediating. It takes a multidimensional model to understand the matrix of trustworthy leadership.

Visioning

If anyone is responsible for lifting up a vision of the school as a trustworthy environment for all constituencies, it is the person charged

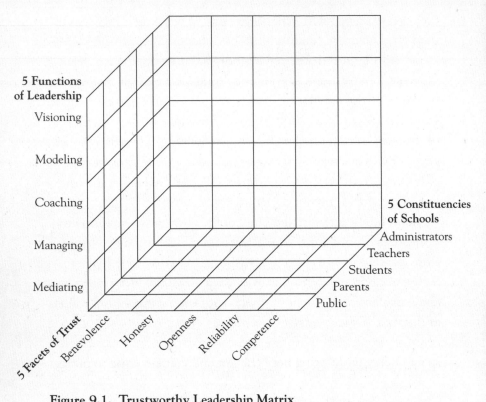

5 Functions of Leadership
Visioning
Modeling
Coaching
Managing
Mediating

5 Constituencies of Schools
Administrators
Teachers
Students
Parents
Public

5 Facets of Trust
Benevolence
Honesty
Openness
Reliability
Competence

Figure 9.1. Trustworthy Leadership Matrix

with the responsibility for school leadership. This exploration of trust gives school leaders a framework from which to speak of trust in dynamic and proactive ways. Once they take stock of the importance of trust to successful schools, they can promote trust before it goes sour. Had Gloria, Fred, and Brenda made use of this framework, it could have made their jobs easier and their leadership more effective.

When Gloria arrived at Lincoln she took over a school in need of change. The students were not being educated well enough to meet even minimal accountability standards. She suspected that members of the faculty were not doing their best for the students of Lincoln. Her vision of turning the school around was an admirable one. But her methods were not. By failing to first establish a benevolent relationship with the people she was charged to work with, her zeal for change came across as judgmental impatience. It damaged the trust with the teachers before it had time to be established.

Even when the principal has taken leadership of a school in which he or she feels that the teachers do not deserve to be trusted, such as in a truly dysfunctional school with negative, cynical attitudes and low expectations for student achievement, the principal is not relieved of the obligation to be trustworthy. There are schools where some teachers actively try to sow discord and distrust toward the administrator, and yet the principal must not retaliate or respond in ways that undermine trust. It is through trustworthy leadership that such situations can best be turned around.

Gloria had a vision for improved student learning at Lincoln School, but in failing to be open and forthcoming with information and plans, Gloria was not seen as trustworthy. Instead of honoring her vision for change, she was suspected of harboring hidden agendas. Instead of working toward the same goal, the teachers spent energy monitoring her behavior and maneuvering to protect themselves—energy that would have been better spent on improving the educational environment at Lincoln.

A better understanding of the relationship between trustworthy leadership and the dynamics of the change process would have enabled Gloria to be more successful in lifting up the vision and "talking the talk" of constructive change at Lincoln (Evans, 1996; Fullan, 2001). She would have structured a process whereby teachers were involved in the vision-casting process, wrestling with the data and developing a plan for addressing deficiencies. This would have laid the foundation for Gloria to be directly engaged with teachers without being disrespectful. She would have been better positioned to assist them to make needed changes.

Modeling

Effective school leaders not only know how to "talk the talk" of trust, they also know how to "walk the talk." If being a role model is ever necessary, it's when it comes to cultivating a culture of trust. Discontinuity between word and example will quickly erode a principal's ability to lead. Setting an example is not to be flaunted. Skillful principals often earn the trust of their faculty by leading *quietly*. They are soft on people and hard on projects. They combine personal humility—exercising restraint and modesty—with tenacity and the professional will to see that the task is accomplished and accomplished well (Collins, 2002; Fullan, 2003).

Fred failed to earn the trust of his faculty because his actions did not reflect his talk of high expectations and stern consequences. In wanting too much to be liked, and in his fear and avoidance of conflict, Fred failed to provide trustworthy leadership for the teachers and students at Fremont. Although Fred genuinely cared about the students and teachers in his school, his lack of leadership left them vulnerable to the mounting problems at the school.

Dealing with problems is where having a framework of trust can assist school leaders to monitor their own behavior and communicate in a straightforward manner. Part of the art of trustworthy leadership is the ability to speak hard truths in a way that communicates value and caring. This takes courage, but it is also more likely to produce constructive change. Trustworthy leaders model norms of conduct that promote the well-being of all members of the school community and explicitly invite others to abide by those norms as well. They defend those norms in ways that make clear that disrespect is not an option.

We see this approach modeled in Brenda's more trustworthy leadership. When Brenda arrived at Brookside, she had many innovative ideas for what she would like to see happening at the school. But Brenda understood wisely that these changes would require extra effort and risk taking on the part of her teachers. She knew she couldn't get there alone. She knew she would need the teachers to be on board, so she was patient and developed relationships. A strategy of small early wins on some key tasks can help build trust in the principal's competence as well as motivation. This builds momentum toward more successful schools.

To consistently serve as a model of trustworthy leadership, it is important for educational leaders to reflect regularly on their words and actions. In the pressure-cooker of a school system, this is a particularly challenging task. Who has the time to STOP—step back, think, and organize their thoughts before proceeding (Gallwey, 2000)? Trustworthy leaders view reflection as a required part of their daily and weekly routines. Brenda arrived at school early, before everyone else, giving her a chance to collect herself at the start of the day. Others engage in regular reflective writing. And school breaks may provide a venue for taking a broader view.

Coaching

Beyond lifting up the vision and modeling the behavior of trustworthy leadership, principals can also build or damage trust by how they engage around the instructional matters of the school. Applying either too much or too little pressure serves to undermine trust and makes principals' leadership of the instructional program less effective.

The school leader as coach is one way to frame and understand the role of instructional leadership that fosters a culture of trust. Coaches assist people to move forward toward their goals through conversation and their way of being with people. They know when to push and when to back off, based on the needs of the situation. They show genuine concern for both the task at hand and the welfare of those who have to accomplish that task. Great coaches epitomize the five facets of trust in their dealings with people.

There is a growing body of research and literature that summarizes the core coaching competencies. These include personal presence, active listening, powerful questioning, creation of awareness, planning and goal setting, design of actions, as well as management of progress and accountability (International Coach Federation,

1999). Mastering these competencies is important for the process of instructional leadership to generate the professional development, self-efficacy beliefs, and enthusiasm of teachers.

Such mastery is predicated on the establishment of trust. As principals issue the challenge to their teachers to find new ways to meet the diverse needs of high-achieving students and those with special needs without neglecting more typical students, those with the trust of their teachers will be more successful at motivating teachers for the extra effort required. Teachers will be more willing to take the risk to try new instructional strategies when a culture of trust pervades the school. In cultivating a professional learning community committed to professional inquiry, data-based decision making, and best practice, as well as helping teachers learn to adapt to new standards of accountability, trustworthy principals can move their schools to higher levels of productivity and success.

Supervision is one aspect of the principal's role as instructional leader in which the establishment of trust and the language of coaching are especially important. Not surprising, trust has been found to play a significant role in employee reactions to supervision. In a study of the perceptions of fairness of performance evaluations by supervisors, the level of trust in the supervisor was more important in regard to perceived fairness than any other characteristics of the performance evaluation process (Fulk, Brief, & Barr, 1985). The traditional norms of schools have allowed teachers a great deal of autonomy and little supervision. Teachers have enjoyed the trust, or at least the neglect, of their supervisors. In the age of accountability, however, this state of affairs is changing. New systems of teacher evaluation require greater inspection of teachers' classroom practice. Greater scrutiny may be perceived as a lessening of trust by both teachers and

WHAT MAKES THE biggest difference is to a have a principal who really listens. When you talk to our principal, he is not really paying attention. You can talk to him later about the same topic and he has no memory of the conversation.

Erika, art teacher

administrators and might in fact lead to less trust. However, if supervision is practiced in such a way that the greater attention is perceived as increased care with a focus on problem solving and coaching, principals will have an opportunity to demonstrate their competence and expertise. Trustworthy leadership is likely to lead to more active and constructive supervision that contributes to improved instruction in the school.

One of the greatest dilemmas faced by school leaders occurs when they don't trust the competence and motivation of their teachers. It is the responsibility of the principal as coach to create the circumstances that extend the sense of purpose and competence of these teachers. The trustworthy principal understands that teachers function within the culture of a school that influences their behavior. If they have worked within a culture that tolerated or even encouraged a slackening of effort, the principal's responses need to take into consideration these environmental factors that have contributed to poor performance.

Because a school culture emerges as a group of people who solve problems together, a principal who wants to change the culture of a school needs to unleash creativity as teachers and administrators alike find new solutions to old problems (Schein, 1992). When a faculty member fails to meet expectations, the principal as coach addresses the issues directly but discretely and in a way that preserves that person's dignity. In this way, teachers can modify their behavior and conform to expectations without compromising their standing or identity in the school community. This coach approach to instructional leadership both stems from and results in a culture of disciplined professional inquiry (Fullan, 2003).

I WAS A struggling new teacher at a school for students with emotional disturbances. I soon learned that if I approached my principal with concerns about a classroom management problem, I would read my own words back to me in my next teacher evaluation. I sought other avenues of support after that.

Bud, special education teacher

Managing

In addition to their role as instructional leader and coach, principals are also charged with the responsibility for management and administration. Here, too, the effective understanding and implementation of the five facets of trust are important to a principal's effectiveness and success. In their managerial capacity, trusting and trustworthy principals will earn critical efficiencies in what is at times an overwhelming task. Principals willing to delegate control will find that they are not so bound by the need to do everything themselves. High-trust principals who have been successful in cultivating a high-trust culture in their schools will find that they need fewer rules and rigid procedures to ensure that teachers are doing what they are supposed to be doing. Greater organizational citizenship will lubricate the smooth functioning of the organization. And principals who have fostered a strong sense of trust with parents and their communities will find that they spend less time explaining their actions and engaging in investigations of the actions of others.

Trustworthy leaders cultivate "a culture of discipline" within their schools in which the norms and expectations support people in being productively engaged with the task so that each person contributes constructively (Collins, 2002). Here, too, principals need to strike a balance in how they handle the rules between how much and how little they push. Gloria pushed too hard. She adopted a manipulative and overly rigid approach to the enforcement of rules. Gloria tried to pressure her teachers through using the teaching contract against them, but this technique did not foster a productive school environment. Fred didn't push hard enough. Fred was not trustworthy because, in his attempts to be supportive and empowering of teachers, he did not confront bad behavior and take action to correct it. Fred lost the trust of his faculty by avoiding conflict and by lax enforcement of rules. Trustworthy principals find the right balance in their handling of policies, rules, and procedures.

They do not abuse their power through manipulation or an over-reliance on a strict interpretation of rules. But neither do they abdicate their responsibility for leadership. Trustworthy principals demonstrate flexibility by focusing more on generating possibilities and solving problems than control. They see rules as means to an end rather than as ends in themselves.

Mediating

Even the most trustworthy of school leaders will have to deal with times of betrayal and conflict in the school environment. But trustworthy principals know how to deal with conflict and repair trust through the process of mediation. For one thing, principals lift up the vision that such repair is possible. In a disposable society known for revolving door relationships, trustworthy school leaders stand for something different. They let all their constituencies know that conflict and even betrayal are not necessarily the last word. They hold out the hope for reconciliation and the repair of trust.

But it's not enough to just lift up a vision, trustworthy leaders must also play the role of mediator when trust breaks down. It is important that the members of the school community, whether students, teachers, or parents, have a trusted resource to turn to when they find themselves in the midst of conflict. Trustworthy school leaders are not only skillful themselves in conflict management

---

WE HAD A problem of stealing. Things were missing—people's lunch from the refrigerator, money from sales would be missing here and there, small items would disappear from your classroom. After we complained to our principal about what was going on, there was an investigation. Then it was announced that a certain staff person would be taking a leave of absence. After that, the problems stopped. We were glad the situation was dealt with but also that it was handled discretely so as not to embarrass anyone.

Jodi, middle school teacher

strategies, but they also create the structures and provide the training for others to improve in this realm. Cultivating more productive ways of dealing with conflict is an important part of building a school culture of trust. Such skills help in restoring trust that has been broken; moreover, they can prevent the breaking of trust in the first place by supporting disputants with norms and processes that help them negotiate solutions that meet the needs of all parties.

Successful Schools

Trustworthy leaders are at the heart of successful schools. Trustworthy leadership gets everyone on the same team, pulling in the same direction. At Brookside, Brenda's trustworthy leadership was contagious; it resulted in more trusting relationships throughout the school community. The faculty clearly came to care for one another. This caring was not limited to small groups of friends within cliques, but extended to every person on the faculty. On a professional level, this faculty looked out for one another, and especially for new teachers. Teachers freely shared ideas and resources. On a personal level, people were also willing to share about their lives outside of school with the expectation that they would receive a caring response. Teachers respected one another's expertise and enjoyed a strong sense of shared commitment to the mission of the school. There was not a sense of competition to outdo one another or to prove who was a better teacher. Teachers were not defensive about their classroom performance. Teachers welcomed one another into their classrooms, whether informally for a visit or to borrow something, or more formally for a peer observation. Teachers were not worried about

WHEN WE TRUSTED teachers to have more say over their time, whether they wanted to teach on the block or not, whether to team, and how they arranged their time within the block, to take breaks when it made sense to them within their lessons, we noticed that it trickled down and that they began to trust their students more too.

Dan, high school principal

being judged harshly or unfairly. They respected each other's integrity and could count on one another to be reliable in their commitments.

Trust was no less important among students and parents. In making trust judgments about children, teachers looked for respect—respect for teachers and other adults, respect for other children, and respect for self. All of the other facets of trust—judgments of honesty, openness, reliability, and competence—seemed to follow from this baseline assessment of respect. Teachers wanted to feel that the parents of their students were as concerned about the children's well-being as they themselves were. They also wanted the parents to believe that teachers had the child's best interests at heart and that they were willing to work together to solve any problems as a team. Teachers also trusted parents who avoided blame but were willing to take responsibility for their own actions. They respected parents who encouraged their children to do the same.

Across the various actors in schools, whether principals, teachers or students, the same facets were important to the cultivation of trust. At its most basic level, trustworthiness had to do with concern for relationships combined with a concern for the task. At the administrative level, this balance was evident in the high-support, high-challenge principal. Among teachers it was expressed as the high-commitment, high-competence teacher. For students, it was the high-respect, high-motivation student. No matter the level within the school community, earning trust had to do with guarding both qualities of care. Trustworthy leadership shows the way through example and by providing the resources, norms, and structures for others to be trustworthy as well. Trustworthy leaders create a culture of trust in their buildings; this trust is at the heart of successful schools.

Putting It into Action

You can make use of the ideas presented in this book to foster greater trust and reap the benefits of greater efficiency, adaptability, and quality in your school. By interfacing the five facets of trust with the five functions of leadership as you relate to the various stakeholders of your school, you will gain new insight and direction as to what needs to be done. Through increased awareness of how trust works and its importance to productive schools, you will be more successful in your job.

When there is a high level of trust in the interpersonal relationships within the school, you and your teachers can celebrate that fact and take action to strengthen the cycle, thereby fostering even greater levels of trust. When there are problems surrounding trust in your school, the model presented in this book can increase your awareness as to the importance of and strategies for fixing those problems. This model can generate new ideas and possibilities, enabling you and your constituents to interrupt the spiral of distrust and begin the journey back to restored trust.

This book can assist you to clearly diagnose the extent of problems with trust by using the Trust Scales available in the Appendix to assess the level of trust in your school. Scoring directions and norms from a broad sample of schools will assist you to capture a snapshot of the trust dynamics at work in your building. You can also make use of additional instruments available through my website (www.MeganTM.com) to assess other aspects of your school, such as the school climate, collective sense of efficacy, and level of organizational citizenship. These instruments can help you map your leadership style as perceived by teachers, as well as the interpersonal interactions among teachers and between teachers and students and the relationship of your school with the community. Once a profile of the school is drawn, you and your teachers can decide whether the trust, climate, and collective efficacy of the school are in need of attention.

These instruments can provide an important window into the perceptions of teachers, students, and parents. Principals are often quite surprised to see that their perceptions of the school are different from those of their teachers. In fact, it is not unusual for principals to describe their schools in more favorable terms than others. The issue then is not who is correct, but to understand the nature of the discrepancy. If teachers perceive the school as low in trust, a place where they have to feel on guard, it is important to know why that is the case and then take appropriate action.

Identifying a lack of trust as a problem is not the same as solving it. There are no quick fixes. The instruments at hand are merely tools for analysis and diagnosis; they cannot solve the problems. But they do provide a basis for examining important features of trust in the school that may be in need of change. Only in conversation with your teachers and other constituents can you solve the problem. Once the diagnosis is made, you will be in a position to engage in a positive strategy of change. The five-facet model of trust presented in this book will generate new commitment, ideas, and strategies for individual coaching, as well as organizational and professional development activities. For example, a problem-solving team can be formed to diagnose the causes of the existing situation, develop an action plan, implement the plan, and assess its success.

Awareness brings with it the responsibility to take constructive action for change. It is the duty of the person with greater power within a hierarchy to accept greater responsibility for the cultivation of trust. Even if you feel wronged and misunderstood, you have the opportunity to work toward renewed trust through being meticulously trustworthy and by announcing these intentions to others. Restoring lost trust is possible, but it is not easy. The effort requires courage, persistence, and forgiveness. The rewards, however, are worth the effort for schools mired in the dysfunctional consequences of a distrustful culture.

Trust is a significant factor in successful schools. Schools that enjoy a culture of trust are likely to benefit from members of the school community willingly working together and going beyond the minimum requirements of their positions. Communication flows more freely when teachers are not afraid of the consequences of candor. A high level of trust helps these schools be wonderful places to learn and grow: a positive, open, and healthy climate pervades the school. The costs of broken trust are great. When distrust pervades a school, constrained communication, poor organizational citizenship, and a proliferation of dysfunctional rules are often the result. Trust matters because it hits school in their bottom line; it makes a difference in student achievement. It is related to teachers' collective sense that they can make a difference and in dealing constructively with conflict. Although the building of trust in schools requires time, effort, and leadership, the investment will bring lasting returns. Trust pays dividends in helping schools succeed at fulfilling their mission to be productive, professional learning communities.

Key Points About Becoming a Trustworthy Leader

- Trustworthy leadership applies the five facets of trust to the five functions of leadership. This multidimensional model can assist educational leaders to proactively foster a culture of trust in their schools. It can also assist them to diagnosis and correct problems of trust before they become insurmountable.

- Trustworthy leaders lift up the vision, model the behavior, provide the coaching, manage the environment, and mediate the breakdowns of trust.

- At all times, trustworthy leaders put the culture of trust ahead of their own ego needs. Skillful principals often earn the trust of their faculty by leading *quietly.*

- Trustworthy principals foster the development of trust in schools by demonstrating flexibility, focusing on problem solving, and involving teachers in important decisions.

- Trustworthy leaders strike the right balance between pushing too hard and pushing too little. They are soft on people and tough on projects. They combine personal humility—exercising restraint and modesty—with tenacity and the professional will to see that the task is accomplished and accomplished well.

- Trust matters to successful leaders and their schools.

Questions for Reflection and Discussion

1. What are some of the costly structures, systems, and practices at your school that could be reduced or eliminated if there was more trust between parents and the school, teachers and administrators, and teachers and students?

2. What is the greatest area in need of attention to trust within your school community? What could you do to improve the level of trust?

Appendixes

Appendix A. Measures of Trust in Schools

Four trust surveys are included in this appendix: surveys for faculty, the principal, parents, and students. The Faculty Trust Survey include three subscales (faculty trust in the principal, faculty trust in colleagues, and faculty trust in students and parents). The Principal Trust Survey contains three subscales (principal trust in teachers, principal trust in students, and principal trust in parents). It is interesting to note that while teachers' trust judgments of students and parents were statistically indistinguishable and had to be combined for analysis, principals' trust judgments of students and parents differed sufficiently to create a separate scale. The Parent Trust Survey includes two subscales (parent trust in the school and parent trust in the principal) and the Student Trust Survey contains only one scale (student trust in the principal). These measures are the result of many years of research. It is my hope that including them will facilitate the further study of trust in schools.

It is critical that ethical standards are adhered to in administering the surveys. The surveys (other than the principal survey) must be administered anonymously so that there is no way for the results to be traced to the individual who completed the survey. Participants should be told that their participation is voluntary and that they may skip any items they are uncomfortable answering. Faculty, parent, and student surveys should be returned to someone other than the principal. Student surveys should be administered outside of class because in a classroom setting students may perceive their completion of the survey to be compulsory, even if they are told their participation is voluntary.

Scoring directions are provided for each of these four surveys, as well as evidence on the reliability and validity of the scales. Directions for calculating a standardized score are included so that schools can compare their results with other schools. The standardized score is presented on a scale with a mean of 500 and a standard deviation of 100, much like an SAT or GRE score. For example, a school with a score of 600 on faculty trust in colleagues is one standard deviation above the average score on faculty trust in colleagues of all schools in the sample. That means that the school has higher faculty trust in colleagues than 84 percent of the schools in the sample.

The range of the standardized scores is presented below:

If the score is 200, it is lower than 99 percent of the schools.

If the score is 300, it is lower than 97 percent of the schools.

If the score is 400, it is lower than 84 percent of the schools.

If the score is 500, it is average.

If the score is 600, it is higher than 84 percent of the schools.

If the score is 700, it is higher than 97 percent of the schools.

If the score is 800, it is higher than 99 percent of the schools.

Ready-to-print versions of these surveys are available at my Web site (www.MeganTM.com) for principals and other practitioners, as well as scholars interested in studying trust in schools.

Exhibit A.1. Faculty Trust Survey

Directions: This questionnaire is designed to help us gain a better understanding of the quality of relationships in schools. Your answers are confidential. Please indicate the extent that you agree or disagree with each of the statements about your school, marking in the columns on the right, ranging from (1) Strongly Disagree to (6) Strongly Agree, filling the bubbles completely.

	Strongly Disagree				*Strongly Agree*	
1. Students in this school care about each other.	①	②	③	④	⑤	⑥
2. Teachers in this school typically look out for each other.	①	②	③	④	⑤	⑥
3. The teachers in this school have faith in the integrity of the principal.	①	②	③	④	⑤	⑥
4. Even in difficult situations, teachers in this school can depend on each other.	①	②	③	④	⑤	⑥
5. The principal in this school typically acts in the best interests of the teachers.	①	②	③	④	⑤	⑥
6. Teachers in this school can rely on the principal.	①	②	③	④	⑤	⑥
7. Teachers in this school trust each other.	①	②	③	④	⑤	⑥
8. Teachers can count on parental support.	①	②	③	④	⑤	⑥
9. Teachers think that most of the parents do a good job.	①	②	③	④	⑤	⑥
10. Teachers in this school trust the principal.	①	②	③	④	⑤	⑥
11. Teachers in this school are open with each other.	①	②	③	④	⑤	⑥
12. Students in this school can be counted on to do their work.	①	②	③	④	⑤	⑥
13. Parents in this school are reliable in their commitments.	①	②	③	④	⑤	⑥
14. The principal doesn't tell teachers what is really going on.	①	②	③	④	⑤	⑥

continued on next page

Exhibit A.1. Faculty Trust Survey, *continued*

	Strongly Disagree					*Strongly Agree*
15. The principal of this school does not show concern for teachers.	①	②	③	④	⑤	⑥
16. Teachers in this school have faith in the integrity of their colleagues.	①	②	③	④	⑤	⑥
17. Teachers in this school trust the parents.	①	②	③	④	⑤	⑥
18. Teachers in this school are suspicious of each other.	①	②	③	④	⑤	⑥
19. Students here are secretive.	①	②	③	④	⑤	⑥
20. When teachers in this school tell you something you can believe it.	①	②	③	④	⑤	⑥
21. Teachers in this school do their jobs well.	①	②	③	④	⑤	⑥
22. Teachers here believe that students are competent learners.	①	②	③	④	⑤	⑥
23. The teachers in this school are suspicious of most of the principal's actions.	①	②	③	④	⑤	⑥
24. Teachers in this school believe what parents tell them.	①	②	③	④	⑤	⑥
25. The principal in this school is competent in doing his or her job.	①	②	③	④	⑤	⑥
26. Teachers in this school trust their students.	①	②	③	④	⑤	⑥

For office use only.

⓪	①	②	③	④	⑤	⑥	⑦	⑧	⑨
⓪	①	②	③	④	⑤	⑥	⑦	⑧	⑨
⓪	①	②	③	④	⑤	⑥	⑦	⑧	⑨

Scoring Directions for Faculty Trust Survey

The Faculty Trust Scale measures the level of faculty trust in a school and consists of three subscales: faculty trust in the principal, faculty trust in colleagues, and faculty trust in clients (students and parents). It can be used at the elementary, middle school or high school levels.

Step 1. Reverse the Response Code of the Items That Are Negatively Worded

Because some items are written as negative rather than positive statements, the response code needs to be reverse, that is [1 = 6, 2 = 5, 3 = 4, 4 = 3, 5 = 2, 6 = 1]. Items to be reverse-coded are identified by an asterisk. For the Faculty Trust Survey, these are items 14, 15, 18, 19, and 23. In this case, because there are six response categories, an easy way to reverse the coding using your statistical package is to program it to rescore each of the selected items by calculating the difference from 7. For example, a score of 5 would be converted to 2 because $7 - 5 = 2$, and a score of 3 would be converted to 4 because $7 - 3 = 4$.

Step 2. Calculate the Average Score for Each Item on the Survey

You will need to calculate the average of all the responses to the survey for each item on the questionnaire. You can use a spreadsheet program such as Microsoft Excel or calculate the means by hand. If you are using a statistical package such as SPSS, you can skip this step and go directly to Step 3 because the package will calculate the mean of the means.

Step 3. Calculate the Mean Score for Your School on Each of the Three Subscales

Use your spreadsheet or statistical package to calculate the school means on each of the subscales.

- Faculty trust in the principal

    $(3 + 5 + 6 + 10 + 14* + 15* + 23* + 25) / 8$

- Faculty trust in colleagues

    $(2 + 4 + 7 + 11 + 16 + 18* + 20 + 21) / 8$

- Faculty trust in clients (students and parents)

    $(1 + 8 + 9 + 12 + 13 + 17 + 19* + 22 + 24 + 26) / 10$

Step 4. Computing the Standardized Scores for the Faculty Trust Scales for Purposes of Comparison

You can convert your school score on each of the subscales to a standardized score with a mean of 500 and a standard deviation of 100 to make comparison with other schools possible. First, compute the difference between your school score on faculty trust of the principal (FTP) and the mean for the normative sample. For a high school, this would mean (FTP − 4.512). Then multiply the difference by one hundred [100(FTP − 4.512)]. Next divide the product by the standard deviation of the normative sample (.662). Then add 500 to the result. You have computed a standardized score for faculty trust in the principal. Repeat the process for each trust dimension as follows, depending on the level of your school:

- For high schools, calculate standardized trust scores using the following formulas:

    Standard score for faculty trust in the principal
    $(FTP) = 100 \, (FTP − 4.512) / .662 + 500$

    Standard score for faculty trust in colleagues
    $(FTT) = 100 \, (FTT − 4.399) / .357 + 500$

    Standard score for faculty trust in clients
    $(FTCl) = 100 \, (FTCl − 3.685) / .349 + 500$

- For middle schools, calculate standardized trust scores using the following formulas:

    Standard score for faculty trust in the principal
    (FTP) = 100 (FTP − 4.606) / .704 + 500

    Standard score for faculty trust in colleagues
    (FTT) = 100 (FTT − 4.204) / .401 + 500

    Standard score for faculty trust in clients
    (FTCl) = 100 (FTCl − 3.42) / .466 + 500

- For elementary schools, calculate standardized trust scores using the following formulas:

    Standard score for faculty trust in the principal
    (FTP) = 100 (FTP − 4.608) / .81 + 500

    Standard score for faculty trust in colleagues
    (FTT) = 100 (FTT − 4.758) / .534 + 500

    Standard score for faculty trust in clients
    (FTCl) = 100 (FTCl − 3.966) / .584 + 500

Reliability and Validity of the Faculty Trust Survey

The norms for the Faculty Trust Survey is based on a sample of ninety-seven high schools in Ohio, sixty-six middle schools in Virginia, and 146 elementary schools in Ohio. The reliabilities of the three subscales typically range from .90 to .98. Factor analytic studies of the Faculty Trust Scale support the construct validity of the measure. For more information on the reliability and validity of the Faculty Trust Survey, see Hoy, W. K., & Tschannen-Moran, M. (2003). The conceptualization and measurement of faculty trust in schools: The omnibus T-Scale. In W. K. Hoy & C. G. Miskel, *Studies in Leading and Organizing Schools* (pp. 181–208). Greenwich, CT: Information Age Publishing.

Exhibit A.2. Principal Trust Survey

Directions: This questionnaire is designed to help us gain a better understanding of the quality of relationships in schools. Your answers are confidential. Please indicate the extent that you agree or disagree with each of the statements about your school, marking in the columns on the right, ranging from (1) Strongly Disagree to (6) Strongly Agree, filling the bubbles completely.

	Strongly Disagree					Strongly Agree
1. Teachers in this school are candid with me.	①	②	③	④	⑤	⑥
2. I can count on parents to support the school.	①	②	③	④	⑤	⑥
3. Students here really care about the school.	①	②	③	④	⑤	⑥
4. I have faith in the integrity of my teachers.	①	②	③	④	⑤	⑥
5. Students in this school can be counted on to do their work.	①	②	③	④	⑤	⑥
6. I believe in my teachers.	①	②	③	④	⑤	⑥
7. Most students in this school are honest.	①	②	③	④	⑤	⑥
8. I question the competence of some of my teachers.	①	②	③	④	⑤	⑥
9. I am often suspicious of teachers' motives in this school.	①	②	③	④	⑤	⑥
10. Most students are able to do the required work.	①	②	③	④	⑤	⑥
11. I trust the students in this school.	①	②	③	④	⑤	⑥
12. When teachers in this school tell you something, you can believe it.	①	②	③	④	⑤	⑥
13. Even in difficult situations, I can depend on my teachers.	①	②	③	④	⑤	⑥
14. Parents in this school have integrity.	①	②	③	④	⑤	⑥
15. Parents in this school are reliable in their commitments.	①	②	③	④	⑤	⑥
16. Most parents openly share information with the school.	①	②	③	④	⑤	⑥

		Strongly Disagree					Strongly Agree

17. My teachers typically look out for me. ① ② ③ ④ ⑤ ⑥

18. I trust the teachers in this school. ① ② ③ ④ ⑤ ⑥

19. Students in this school are reliable. ① ② ③ ④ ⑤ ⑥

20. Most parents here have good
parenting skills. ① ② ③ ④ ⑤ ⑥

For office use only.

⓪ ① ② ③ ④ ⑤ ⑥ ⑦ ⑧ ⑨

⓪ ① ② ③ ④ ⑤ ⑥ ⑦ ⑧ ⑨

⓪ ① ② ③ ④ ⑤ ⑥ ⑦ ⑧ ⑨

Scoring Directions for Principal Trust Survey

The Principal Trust Survey measures the level of principal trust in three constituencies: principal trust in the faculty, principal trust of students, and principal trust in parents.

Step 1. Reverse the Response Code of the Items That Are Negatively Worded

Because some items are written as negative rather than positive statements, the response code needs to be reverse, that is [1 = 6, 2 = 5, 3 = 4, 4 = 3, 5 = 2, 6 = 1]. Items to be reverse-coded are identified by an asterisk. For the Principal Trust Survey, these are items 8 and 9. Because there are six response categories, an easy way to reverse the coding by using your statistical package is to program it to rescore each of the selected items by calculating the difference from 7. For example, a score of 5 would be converted to 2 because $7 - 5 = 2$, and a score of 3 would be converted to 4 because $7 - 3 = 4$.

Step 2. Calculate the Average Score for Each Item on the Survey

You will need to calculate the average of all the responses to the survey for each item on the questionnaire. You can use a spreadsheet program such as Microsoft Excel or calculate the means by hand. If you are using a statistical package such as SPSS, you can skip this step and go directly to Step 3 because the package will calculate the mean of the means.

Step 3. Calculate the Mean Score for Your School on Each of the Three Subscales

Use your spreadsheet or statistical package to calculate the school means on each of the subscales:

- Principal trust in teachers

  $(1 + 4 + 6 + 8* + 9* + 12 + 13 + 17 + 18) / 9$

- Principal trust in clients (students and parents)

  $(3 + 5 + 7 + 10 + 11 + 19) / 6$

- Principal trust in parents

  $(2 + 14 + 15 + 16 + 20) / 5$

Step 4. Computing the Standardized Scores for the Principal Trust Survey for Purposes of Comparison

You can convert your school score on each of the subscales to a standardized score with a mean of 500 and a standard deviation of 100 to make comparison with other schools possible. First compute the difference between your school score on principal trust of teachers (PTT) and the mean for the normative sample (PTT – 4.911). Then multiply the difference by 100 [100(PTT – 4.911)]. Next divide the product by the standard deviation of the normative sample (.618). Then add 500 to the result. You have computed a standardized score for principal trust in teachers. Repeat the process for each subscale as follows:

- For principal trust in teachers, calculate a standardized trust score using the following formula:

Standard score for principal trust in teachers
(PTT) = 100 (PTT − 4.911) / .618 + 500

- For principal trust in students, calculate a standardized trust score using the following formula:

standard score for principal trust in students
(PTS) = 100 (PTS − 4.827) / .587 + 500

- For principal trust in parents, calculate a standardized trust score using the following formula:

Standard score for principal trust in parents
(PTP) = 100(PTP − 4.502)/.719 + 500

Reliability and Validity of the Principal Trust Survey

The norms are based on a sample of 642 principals in Virginia and Ohio. The reliability for principal trust in teachers was .87 in the norming sample, .87 for principal trust in students, and .86 for principal trust in parents. Factor analytic studies of the Principal Trust Scale support the construct validity of this measure. For more information, see Gareis, C. R., & Tschannen-Moran, M. (2004, April). *Principals' Sense of Efficacy and Trust*. Paper presented at the annual meeting of the American Educational Research Association, San Diego.

Exhibit A.3. Parent Trust Survey

Directions: This questionnaire is designed to help us gain a better understanding of the quality of relationships in schools. Your answers are confidential. Please indicate the extent that you agree or disagree with each of the statements about your school, marking in the columns on the right, ranging from (1) Strongly Disagree to (8) Strongly Agree, filling the bubbles completely.

	Strongly Disagree						*Strongly Agree*	
1. This school is always ready to help.	①	②	③	④	⑤	⑥	⑦	⑧
2. This school has high standards for all kids.	①	②	③	④	⑤	⑥	⑦	⑧
3. This school keeps me well informed.	①	②	③	④	⑤	⑥	⑦	⑧
4. Kids at this school are well cared for.	①	②	③	④	⑤	⑥	⑦	⑧
5. This school always does what it is supposed to.	①	②	③	④	⑤	⑥	⑦	⑧
6. At this school, I know I'll be listened to.	①	②	③	④	⑤	⑥	⑦	⑧
7. I never worry about my child when he/she's there.	①	②	③	④	⑤	⑥	⑦	⑧
8. This school is always honest with me.	①	②	③	④	⑤	⑥	⑦	⑧
9. This school does a terrific job.	①	②	③	④	⑤	⑥	⑦	⑧
10. I really trust this school.	①	②	③	④	⑤	⑥	⑦	⑧

The Principal of the school . . .

11. treats everyone with respect.	①	②	③	④	⑤	⑥	⑦	⑧
12. is always ready to help.	①	②	③	④	⑤	⑥	⑦	⑧
13. is good at his/her job.	①	②	③	④	⑤	⑥	⑦	⑧
14. has high standards for all students.	①	②	③	④	⑤	⑥	⑦	⑧
15. is always there when you need him/her.	①	②	③	④	⑤	⑥	⑦	⑧
16. keeps an open door.	①	②	③	④	⑤	⑥	⑦	⑧
17. is always honest.	①	②	③	④	⑤	⑥	⑦	⑧
18. knows how to make learning happen.	①	②	③	④	⑤	⑥	⑦	⑧
19. can be counted on to do his/her job.	①	②	③	④	⑤	⑥	⑦	⑧

	Strongly Disagree							Strongly Agree
20. invites both criticism and praise from parents.	①	②	③	④	⑤	⑥	⑦	⑧
21. owns up to his/her mistakes.	①	②	③	④	⑤	⑥	⑦	⑧
22. is well intentioned.	①	②	③	④	⑤	⑥	⑦	⑧
23. likes to talk to parents.	①	②	③	④	⑤	⑥	⑦	⑧
24. is very reliable.	①	②	③	④	⑤	⑥	⑦	⑧
25. is trustworthy.	①	②	③	④	⑤	⑥	⑦	⑧

For office use only.
⓪ ① ② ③ ④ ⑤ ⑥ ⑦ ⑧ ⑨
⓪ ① ② ③ ④ ⑤ ⑥ ⑦ ⑧ ⑨
⓪ ① ② ③ ④ ⑤ ⑥ ⑦ ⑧ ⑨

Scoring Directions for Parent Trust Survey

The Parent Trust Scale measures two aspects of parent trust: parent trust in the school and parent trust of the principal.

Step 1. Calculate the Average Score for Each Item on the Survey

You will need to calculate the average of all the responses to the survey for each item on the questionnaire. You can use a spreadsheet program such as Microsoft Excel or calculate the means by hand. If you are using a statistical package such as SPSS, you can skip this step and go directly to Step 3 because the package will calculate the mean of the means.

Step 2. Calculate the Mean Score for Your School on Each of the Two Subscales

Use your spreadsheet or statistical package to calculate the school means on each of the subscales.

- Parent trust in the school

    $(1 + 2 + 3 + 4 + 5 + 6 + 7 + 8 + 9 + 10) / 10$

- Parent trust in the principal

    $(11 + 12 + 13 + 14 + 15 + 16 + 17 + 18 + 19 + 20 +$
    $21 + 22 + 23 + 24 + 25) / 15$

Step 3. Computing the Standardized Scores for the Parent Trust Survey for Purposes of Comparison

You can convert your school score on each of the subscales to a standardized score with a mean of 500 and a standard deviation of 100 to make comparison with other schools possible. First compute the difference between your school score on parent trust of the school (PaTS) and the mean for the normative sample (PaTS − 5.78). Then multiply the difference by 100 [100(PTT − 5. 78)]. Next divide the product by the standard deviation of the normative sample (1.68). Then add 500 to the result. You have computed a standardized score for parent trust in the school. Repeat the process for parent trust in the principal, using the second formula. Calculate standardized trust scores for parent trust using the following formulas:

Standard score for parent trust in the school
$(PaTS) = 100 \, (PaTS − 5.78) / 1.68 + 500$

Standard score for parent trust in the principal
$(PaTP) = 100(PaTP − 5.8)/1.68 + 500$

Reliability and Validity of the Parent Trust Survey

The norms are based on the responses of 428 parents for parent trust in schools and 417 parents for parent trust in principal. The reliabilities for these measures among the norming sample were .95 for parent trust in the school and .97 for parent trust in the principal. For more information on the Parent Trust Survey, see Forsyth, P. B.,

& Adams, C. M. (2004). Social capital in education: Taking stock of concept and measure. In W. K. Hoy & C. G. Miskel, *Studies in Leading and Organizing Schools* (Volume 4, in press). Greenwich, CT: Information Age Publishing.

Exhibit A.4. Student Trust Survey

Directions: Please tell us how much you agree or disagree with each of the statements about your school. Fill in the bubbles on the right, choosing from (1) Strongly Disagree, (2) Disagree, (3) Agree, or (4) Strongly Agree.

	Strongly Disagree	Disagree	Agree	Strongly Agree
The Principal at my school . . .				
1. likes students	①	②	③	④
2. is fair	①	②	③	④
3. is there for students	①	②	③	④
4. does his/her job well	①	②	③	④
5. makes me feel safe	①	②	③	④
6. tells the truth to students	①	②	③	④
7. does the right thing	①	②	③	④
8. treats students with respect	①	②	③	④
9. is helpful	①	②	③	④
10. is smart	①	②	③	④
11. is nice	①	②	③	④
12. can be trusted	①	②	③	④

For office use only.

⓪ ① ② ③ ④ ⑤ ⑥ ⑦ ⑧ ⑨
⓪ ① ② ③ ④ ⑤ ⑥ ⑦ ⑧ ⑨
⓪ ① ② ③ ④ ⑤ ⑥ ⑦ ⑧ ⑨

Scoring Directions for Student Trust Survey

Step 1. Calculate the Average Score for Each Item on the Survey

You will need to calculate the average of all the responses to the survey for each item on the questionnaire. You can use a spreadsheet program such as Microsoft Excel or calculate the means by hand. If you are using a statistical package such as SPSS, you can skip this step and go directly to Step 3 because the package will calculate the mean of the means.

Step 2. Calculate the Mean Score of Student Trust in the Principal for Your School

Use your spreadsheet or statistical package to calculate the school mean of all twelve items.

Step 3. Computing the Standardized Scores for the Student Trust Survey for Purposes of Comparison

You can convert your school score to a standardized score with a mean of 500 and a standard deviation of 100 to make comparison with other schools possible. First compute the difference between your school score on student trust in the principal (STP) and the mean for the normative sample. For a high school, this would mean (STP – 3.08). Then multiply the difference by 100 [100 (STP – 3.08)]. Next divide the product by the standard deviation of the normative sample (.36). Then add 500 to the result. You have computed a standardized score for student trust in the principal. For middle school or elementary schools, use the appropriate formula below. Remember that the student trust survey has a four-point response scale.

- For high schools, calculate standardized trust scores using the following formulas:

  Standard score for student trust in the principal
  (STP) = 100 (STP – 3.08) / .36 + 500

- For middle schools, calculate standardized trust scores using the following formulas:

  Standard score for student trust in the principal (STP) = 100 (STP − 3.49) / .34 + 500

- For elementary schools, calculate standardized trust scores using the following formulas:

  Standard score for student trust in the principal (STP) = 100_(STP − 3.64)/.22 + 500

Reliability and Validity of the Student Trust Survey

The norms are based on twenty-two elementary schools, thirty middle schools, and twenty-seven high schools in Oklahoma. For more information, see Forsyth, P. B., & Adams, C. M. (2004). Social capital in education: Taking stock of concept and measure. In W. K. Hoy & C. G. Miskel, *Studies in Leading and Organizing Schools* (Volume 4, in press). Greenwich, CT: Information Age Publishing; Barnes, L.L.B., Adams, C. M., & Forsyth, P. B. (2004, April). *Student trust of principal: Instrument development.* Paper presented at the annual meeting of the American Educational Research Association, San Diego.

Appendix B. Guide to Principals for Presenting Results of the Trust Surveys to Your Faculty

The study of trust has been likened to the study of the roots of a delicate plant. Without great care, the examination can damage or even destroy the very thing about which greater understanding is sought. Consequently, I urge caution in the use of these trust scales. Although they can be powerful tools in helping to reveal the underlying dynamics of trust in the relationships within your school, they can do more harm than good if the information is not handled with sensitivity and care. If these data reveal that there are problems in the patterns of trust within your building, there is no better time to begin to exercise trustworthy behavior than in the presentation of these results.

Although these tools hold the possibility of improving the productivity and effectiveness of your school by identifying areas in need of improved trust, the revelation of distrust or even less than optimal trust can be hard to take. Principals have described feeling hurt and disappointed, even like they have been "kicked in the stomach," on receiving results that reveal a lack of trust in their leadership. Teachers may have similar feelings. It is important not to lash out in reaction to this perceived insult but to seek to understand the perceptions and feelings that are revealed on the surveys. If you don't want to know the truth, don't administer the surveys in the first place. You can be glad for the opportunity to get a window into others' thinking that might not otherwise be available to you. Suppressing negative results will only lead to greater distrust, so do not administer the surveys if you do not intend to share the results with those who offered their opinions.

One thing to keep in mind about the scoring norms is that a score of less than 500 does not necessarily mean that the respondents have indicated distrust of you or others. They may, in fact, have tended to agree more than disagree with the positive statements on the survey but still come out with a standardized score of less than the mean. A score below 500 simply means that the average trust rating at your school was not as high as the average for the larger sample of schools on which the norms were based. For example, the mean score for faculty trust in the principal at the elementary and middle school level is 4.6. A mean score within your school of 4.5, or halfway between slightly agree and somewhat agree, would result in a score that was nonetheless below 500.

In presenting the results of the surveys to the faculty or other stakeholders, it is important to avoid blaming or looking for scapegoats. This is the time for openness, vulnerability, and authenticity. It is time for open-minded curiosity about how things got to be the way they are, followed by a conversation about how participants would like for them to be and about how to make that happen. Compelling evidence on the importance of trust to high-performing schools has been presented in this book. If your scores indicate there is a problem with trust in your building, you have the opportunity to make addressing these concerns a priority.

Appendix C. Study Participants

Identifying Study Participants

The three schools in this study were selected based on reputation and the knowledge of a district insider. Their designation as high- or low-trust schools was confirmed by a quantitative study that assessed a large sample of schools in the same urban district by using the faculty trust survey presented in Appendix A. Brookside was in the top quartile of schools, whereas both Fremont and Lincoln were in the bottom quartile. The informant helped identify a diverse sample of teachers from the three schools who varied along three dimensions: novice-veteran, black-white, male-female.

Note: Some of the interview data in Chapter Six was from another principal, not Brenda, but one whose leadership style was similar to Brenda's. These data were attributed to Brenda to facilitate the readability of the text. Their inclusion makes the description of Brenda a composite prototype.

Table C.1. Study Participants

School, Participants	Novice	Veteran	Black	White	Male	Female
Brookside						
Kathy	*			*		*
Christy		*	*			*
David		*	*		*	
Brenda		*		*		*
Lincoln						
Allisha	*		*			*
Mary		*		*		*
Rob		*		*	*	
Gloria		*	*			*
Fremont						
Brian	*			*	*	
Kelli		*		*		*
Paul		*		*	*	
Fred		*	*		*	

Appendix D. Directions for Future Research

Research on trust in the school context is just beginning. There are a host of unanswered issues and questions. It is clear that trust is a salient aspect of school life. It is an important end in itself. There is also a growing body of evidence that suggests that trust is related to other important outcomes such as student achievement and other measures of organizational productivity. Greater understanding of the practices that foster trust are likely to result in more effective school functioning. Both quantitative and qualitative studies of trust and trustworthy leadership in schools are needed. Qualitative studies are helpful in exploring the dynamic nature of trust within particular school buildings. Quantitative studies are needed to explore the various facets of trust and their relationship to other constructs across a large number of schools. A few illustrative examples of areas in need of further study are offered below.

More work could be done in understanding the dynamics of trustworthy leadership. For example, studies that reveal how trust is fostered when a new principal or superintendent enters a school setting would be useful. What strategies do expert principals employ for establishing trust with a new faculty? What impact does the existing level of trust in a building make on the decisions and strategies of a new principal coming into that building? How is the level of faculty trust related to the principal's sense of efficacy? Once established, how is the level of trust linked to leader effectiveness and the leader's ability to lead change initiatives? To what extent is faculty trust in the principal related to teachers' propensity to innovate and take risks?

The development of faculty trust is another area in need of inquiry. What is the impact of a school's culture of trust on new faculty members in realms such as their commitment, satisfaction, and motivation? To what extent is faculty trust in the principal and in one another related to teachers' sense of efficacy or the collective sense of efficacy of the faculty as a whole? What do principals do to cultivate faculty trust in colleagues? What kinds of school structures facilitate faculty trust? As teachers collaborate more, what communication and conflict resolution skills are needed to nurture greater teacher trust in one another?

The study of student trust has also been neglected. There is intriguing evidence that trust matters in facilitating student learning, yet we know little about the structural, cultural, and individual characteristics of teachers and schools that promote student trust. For example, do school structures such as academic teams and block scheduling cultivate greater student trust? What kind of teacher and student values and norms foster student trust? Are certain teaching styles more or less conducive to the development of student trust? A climate of academic press, meaning the seriousness with which academics are regarded within a school community, seems critical in promoting higher levels of achievement, but what role does trust play in fostering the mechanisms that translate a high level of academic press into higher levels of student performance? To what extent do high levels of academic press and trust in a school promote teacher and student persistence to learning goals? How do schools with high faculty trust in students and parents help overcome some of the disadvantage of low socioeconomic status with respect to student achievement? To what extent is faculty trust in clients an important aspect of communication, collaboration, and cooperation with parents?

Knowledge of the facets and dynamics of trust is also important in understanding the linkages between organizational levels in schools: between boards and superintendents, between superintendents and principals, between principals and teachers, between teachers and students, and between parents and schools. Understanding trust within organizational levels is also important: teacher to teacher as well as student to student relationships.

One of the reasons that an urban district was chosen as the study site in this book was because it was expected that diversity and the mobility of students would be factors in the trust relationships found. Previous research has suggested that trust is more difficult in situations of diversity because people are uncertain about the cultural norms of others (Kipnis, 1996) and are likely to stereotype outgroup members more readily and negatively (Mullen & Hu, 1989). In addition, because trust takes time to develop and requires knowledge and experience with a person over a period of time, it was expected that a high rate of mobility would be detrimental to the development of trust. Greater exploration of the factors of cultivating trust in the midst of cultural and economic diversity, as well as in situations of mobility, would help highlight these important influences on trust.

Another significant series of research questions revolves around the conditions that are necessary to facilitate the emergence of trust within the societal context of the accountability movement. To what extent do recent efforts to make schools more accountable to the public impede or enhance the development of trust? Research questions abound. To what extent is trust related to power and politics? To constructive and destructive conflict? To shared decision making? To innovation and change? We are just beginning to scratch the surface of the study of trust in schools. The questions concerning how trust functions in the context of schools are important as schools struggle to rise to the challenge of a changed and changing world. The four decades of research upon which this book is based lay a solid conceptual and empirical foundation for continuing the quest to understand trust in schools.

References

Adams, K. S., & Christenson, S. L. (2000). Trust and the family-school relationship: Examination of parent-teacher differences in elementary and secondary grades. *Journal of School Psychology, 38,* 477–497.

Adler, P. S., & Borys, B. (1996). Two types of bureaucracy: Enabling and coercive. *Administrative Quarterly, 41,* 61–89.

Allinder, R. M. (1994). The relationship between efficacy and the instructional practices of special education teachers and consultants. *Teacher Education and Special Education, 17*(2), 86–95.

Allison, S. T., & Messick, D. M. (1985). The group attribution error. *Journal of Experimental Social Psychology, 21,* 563–579.

Anderson, R. N., Greene, M. L., & Loewen, P. S. (1988). Relationships among teachers' and students' thinking skills, sense of efficacy, and student achievement. *The Alberta Journal of Educational Research, 34*(2), 148–165.

Armor, D., Conry-Oseguera, P., Cox, M., King, M., McDonnell, L., Pascal, A., Pauly, E., & Zellmann, G. (1976). *Analysis of the school preferred reading program in selected Los Angeles Minority Schools.* Santa Monica, CA: Rand Corporation.

Arrow, K. J. (1974). *The limits of organization.* New York: Norton.

Ashton, P. T., & Webb, R. B. (1986). Teachers' sense of efficacy, classroom behavior, and student achievement. In P. T. Ashton & R. B. Webb (Eds.), *Teachers' sense of efficacy and student achievement* (pp. 125–144). New York & London: Longman.

Baier, A. C. (1994). *Moral prejudices.* Cambridge, MA: Harvard University Press.

Bandura, A. (1993). Perceived self-efficacy in cognitive development and functioning. *Educational Psychologist, 28*(2), 117–148.

Bandura, A. (1997). *Self-efficacy: The exercise of control.* New York: Freeman.

Barber, B. (1983). *The logic and limits of trust*. New Brunswick, NJ: Rutgers University Press.

Barnes, L.L.B., Adams, C. M., & Forsyth, P. B. (2004, April). *Student trust of principal: Instrument development*. Paper presented at the annual meeting of the American Educational Research Association, San Diego.

Barney, J. B., & Hansen, M. H. (1994). Trustworthiness as a source of competitive advantage. *Strategic Management Journal, 15*, 175–190.

Baron, R. A. (1997). Positive effects of conflict: Insights from social cognition. In C.K.W. De Dreu & E. Van de Vliert (Eds.), *Using conflict in organizations* (pp. 101–115). Thousand Oaks, CA: Sage.

Barth, R. (1981, Spring). The principal as staff developer. *Journal of Education, 144*–163.

Berg, J., Dickhaut, J., & McCabe, K. (1995). *Trust, reciprocity, and social history*. Unpublished working paper, University of Minnesota, Minneapolis.

Berliner, D. C., & Biddle, B. J. (1995). *The manufactured crisis: Myths, fraud, and the attack on America's public schools*. Reading, MA: Addison-Wesley.

Bies, R. J., & Tripp, T. M. (1996). Beyond distrust: "Getting even" and the need for revenge. In R. Kramer & T. Tyler (Eds.), *Trust in organizations* (pp. 246–260). Thousand Oaks, CA: Sage.

Bigley, G. A., & Pearce, J. L. (1998). Straining for shared meaning in organization science: Problems of trust and distrust. *Academy of Management Review, 23*, 405–421.

Blake, M., & MacNeil, A. J. (1998). Trust: The quality required for successful management. In Y. Cano, F. H. Wood, & J. C. Simmons (Eds.), *Creating high functioning schools: Practice and research* (pp. 29–37). Springfield, IL: Charles C. Thomas.

Brewer, M. B. (1995). In-group favoritism: The subtle side of intergroup discrimination. In D. M. Messick & A. Tenbrunsel (Eds.), *Behavioral research and business ethics* (pp. 101–117). New York: Russell Sage Foundation.

Bryk, A. S., & Schneider, B. (2002). *Trust in schools: A core resource for school improvement*. New York: Russell Sage Foundation.

Burt, R. S., & Knez, M. (1996). Trust and third-party gossip. In R. Kramer & T. Tyler (Eds.), *Trust in organizations* (pp. 68–89). Thousand Oaks, CA: Sage.

Butler, J. K. (1991). Towards understanding and measuring conditions of trust: Evolution of a conditions of trust inventory. *Journal of Management, 17*, 643–663.

Butler, J. K., & Cantrell, R. S. (1984). A behavioral decision theory approach to modeling dyadic trust in superiors and subordinates. *Psychological Reports, 55*, 81–105.

Coach U, Inc. (2003). *Personal foundation—Level 2*. Steamboat Springs, CO: Coach U, Inc.

Coleman, J. S. (1990). *Foundations of social theory*. Cambridge, MA: Belknap Press of Harvard University Press.

Collins, J. (2002). *Good to great: Why some companies make the leap . . . and others don't*. New York: HarperBusiness.

Creed, W.E.D., & Miles, R. E. (1996). Trust in organizations: A conceptual framework linking organizational forms, managerial philosophies, and the opportunity costs of controls. In R. Kramer & T. Tyler (Eds.), *Trust in organizations* (pp. 16–38). Thousand Oaks, CA: Sage.

Cummings, L. L., & Bromily, P. (1996). The Organizational Trust Inventory (OTI): Development and validation. In R. Kramer & T. Tyler (Eds.), *Trust in organizations* (pp. 302– 330). Thousand Oaks, CA: Sage.

Dasgupta, P. (1988). Trust as a commodity. In D. Gambetta (Ed.), *Trust: Making and breaking cooperative relations* (pp. 213– 238). Cambridge, MA: Basil Blackwell.

Deluga, R. J. (1994). Supervisor trust building, leader-member exchange and organizational citizenship behavior. *Journal of Occupational and Organizational Psychology, 67,* 315.

Deutsch, M. (1960). The effect of motivational orientation upon trust and suspicion. *Human Relations, 13,* 123–139.

Deutsch, M. (2000). Cooperation and competition. In M. Deutsch & P. T. Coleman (Eds.), *The handbook of conflict resolution: Theory and practice* (pp. 21–40). San Francisco: Jossey-Bass.

Elangovan, A. R., & Shapiro, D. L. (1998). Betrayal of trust in organizations. *Academy of Management Review, 23,* 547–566.

Elmore, R. F., Peterson, P. L., & McCarthey, S. J. (1996). *Restructuring the classroom: Teaching, learning, and school organization*. San Francisco: Jossey-Bass.

Evans, R. (1996). *The human side of change: Reform, resistance, and real-life problems of innovation*. San Francisco: Jossey-Bass.

Fisher, R., & Brown, S. (1988). *Getting together*. Boston: Houghton Mifflin.

Forsyth, P. B., & Adams, C. M. (2004). Social capital in education: Taking stock of concept and measure. In W. K. Hoy & C. G. Miskel (Eds.), *Studies in leading and organizing schools* (Volume 4, in press). Greenwich, CT: Information Age Publishing.

Fox, A. (1974). *Beyond contract: Work, power and trust relations*. London: Farber & Farber.

Fukuyama, F. (1995). *Trust: The social virtues and the creation of prosperity*. New York: Simon & Schuster.

Fulk, J., Brief, A. P., & Barr, S. H. (1985). Trust in the supervisor and perceived fairness and accuracy of performance evaluations. *Journal of Business Research, 13,* 301–313.

Fullan, M. (2001). *Leading in a culture of change.* San Francisco: Jossey-Bass.

Fullan, M. (2003). *The moral imperative of school leadership.* Thousand Oaks, CA: Corwin.

Gabarro, J. J. (1978). The development of trust, influence, and expectations. In A. G. Athos & J. J. Gabarro (Eds.), *Interpersonal behavior: Communication and understanding in relationships* (pp. 290–303). Englewood Cliffs, NJ: Prentice Hall.

Gallwey, W. T. (2000). *The inner game of work.* New York: Random House.

Gareis, C. R., & Tschannen-Moran, M. (2004, April). *Principals' sense of efficacy and trust.* Paper presented at the annual meeting of the American Educational Research Association, San Diego.

Gibson, S., & Dembo, M. H. (1984). Teacher efficacy: A construct validation. *Journal of Educational Psychology, 76*(4), 569–582.

Goddard, R. D., Hoy, W. K., & Woolfolk Hoy, A. (2001). Collective teacher efficacy: Its meaning, measure, and impact on student achievement. *American Educational Research Journal, 37,* 479–508.

Goddard, R. D., Tschannen-Moran, M., & Hoy, W. K. (2001). A multilevel examination of the distribution and effects of teacher trust in students and parents in urban elementary schools. *Elementary School Journal, 102* (1), 3–17.

Goldring, E. B., & Rallis, S. F. (1993). *Principals of dynamic schools: Taking charge of change.* Thousand Oaks, CA: Corwin.

Goodlad, J. I. (1984). *A place called school: Prospects for the future.* New York: McGraw-Hill.

Govier, T. (1992). Distrust as a practical problem. *Journal of Social Philosophy, 23,* 52–63.

Greenberg, J. (1993). The social side of fairness: Interpersonal and informational classes of organizational justice. In R. Cropanzano (Ed.), *Justice in the workplace* (pp. 79–103). Hillsdale, NJ: Erlbaum.

Gulati, R. (1995). Does familiarity breed trust? The implications of repeated ties for contractual choice in alliances. *Academy of Management Journal, 38,* 85–112.

Harris, G. G. (1994). *Trust and betrayal in the workplace.* Unpublished doctoral dissertation, University of Utah, Salt Lake City.

Henderson, J. E. & Hoy, W. K. (1982). Principal authenticity, school climate, and pupil-control orientation. *Alberta Journal of Educational Research, 2,* 123–130.

Hirschhorn, L. (1997). Reworking authority: Leading and following in a post-modern organization. Cambridge, MA: MIT Press.

Hocker, J. L., & Wilmot, W. W. (1985). *Interpersonal conflict* (2nd ed.). Dubuque, IA: William C. Brown.

Hoy, W. K., Blazovsky, R., & Newland, W. (1983). Bureaucracy and alienation: A comparative analysis. *Journal of Educational Administration, 21,* 109–120.

Hoy, W. K., & Kupersmith, W. J. (1985). The meaning and measure of faculty trust. *Educational and Psychological Research, 5,* 1–10.

Hoy, W. K., & Miskel, C. G. (2001). *Educational administration: Theory, research, practice.* Boston: McGraw-Hill.

Hoy, W. K., & Sweetland, S. R. (2000). Bureaucracies that work: Enabling not coercive. *Journal of School Leadership, 10,* 525–541.

Hoy, W. K., & Sweetland, S. R. (2001). Designing better schools: The meaning and nature of enabling school structure. *Educational Administration Quarterly, 37,* 296–321.

Hoy, W. K. & Tarter, C. J. (2003). *Administrators solving the problems of practice: Decision-making, concepts, cases, and consequences.* Boston: Allyn & Bacon.

Hoy, W. K., & Tschannen-Moran, M. (1999). Five faces of trust: An empirical confirmation in urban elementary schools. *Journal of School Leadership, 9,* 184–208.

Hoy, W. K. & Tschannen-Moran, M. (2003). The conceptualization and measurement of faculty trust in schools: The omnibus T-Scale. In W. K. Hoy & C. G. Miskel (Eds.), *Studies in leading and organizing schools* (pp. 181–208). Greenwich, CT: Information Age Publishing.

International Coach Federation, (1999). Core coaching competencies. Retrieved January 9, 2004. http://www.coachfederation.org/credentialing/en/core.htm.

Janis, I. L. (1982). *Groupthink: Psychological studies of policy decisions and fiascos.* Boston: Houghton Mifflin.

Johnson-George, C. E., & Swap, W. C. (1982). Measurement of specific interpersonal trust: Construction and validation of a scale to assess trust in a specific other. *Journal of Personality and Social Psychology, 43,* 1306–1317.

Jones, G. R., & George, J. M. (1998). The experience and evolution of trust: Implications for cooperation and teamwork. *Academy of Management Review, 23,* 531–546.

Jones, W., & Burdette, M. P. (1994). Betrayal in relationships. In A. Weber & J. Harvey (Eds.), *Perspectives on close relationships* (pp. 243–262). Boston: Allyn & Bacon.

Kipnis, D. (1996). Trust and technology. In R. Kramer & T. Tyler (Eds.), *Trust in organizations* (pp. 39–50). Thousand Oaks, CA: Sage.

Klayman, J., & Ha, Y. W. (1997). Confirmation, disconfirmation, and information in hypothesis testing. In W. M. Goldstein & R. M. Hogarth (Eds.), *Research on judgment and decision making: Currents, connections, and controversies*. Cambridge: Cambridge University Press.

Konovsky, M. A., & Pugh, S. D. (1994). Citizenship behavior and social exchange. *Academy of Management Review, 37*, 656–669.

Kozol, J. (1991). *Savage inequalities: Children in America's schools*. New York: Crown Publishers.

Kramer, R. M. (1996). Divergent realities and convergent disappointments in the hierarchic relation: Trust and the intuitive auditor at work. In R. Kramer & T. Tyler (Eds.), *Trust in organizations* (pp. 216–245). Thousand Oaks, CA: Sage.

Kramer, R. M., Brewer, M. B., & Hanna, B. A. (1996). Collective trust and collective action: The decision to trust as a social decision. In R. Kramer & T. Tyler (Eds.), *Trust in organizations* (pp. 357–389). Thousand Oaks, CA: Sage.

Kratzer, C. C. (1997, March). *A community of respect, caring, and trust: One school's story*. Paper presented at the annual meeting of the American Educational Research Association, Chicago.

Lareau, A. (1987). Social class differences in family-school relationships: The importance of cultural capital. *Sociology of Education, 60*, 73–85.

Leonard, P. E. (1999, November). *Do teachers value collaboration? The impact of trust*. Paper presented at the annual meeting of the University Council for Educational Administration, Minneapolis, MN.

Lewicki, R. J., & Bunker, B. B. (1996). Developing and maintaining trust in work relationships. In R. Kramer & T. Tyler (Eds.), *Trust in organizations* (pp. 114–139). Thousand Oaks, CA: Sage.

Lewicki, R. J., McAllister, D. J., & Bies, R. J. (1998). Trust and distrust: New relationships and realities. *Academy of Management Review, 23*, 438–458.

Lewis, J. D., & Weigert, A. (1985). Trust as a social reality. *Social Forces, 63*, 967–985.

Limerick, D., & Cunnington, B. (1993). *Managing the new organization*. San Francisco: Jossey-Bass.

Lindskold, S., & Bennett, R. (1973). Attributing trust and conciliatory intent from coercive power capability. *Journal of Personality and Social Psychology, 28*, 180–186.

Little, J. W. (1990). The persistence of privacy: Autonomy and initiative in teachers' professional relations. *Teachers College Record, 91*, 509–536.

Louis, K. S., Kruse, S., & Associates. (1995). *Professionalism and community: Perspectives on reforming urban schools.* Thousand Oaks, CA: Corwin.

Louis, K. S., Kruse, S., & Marks, H. M. (1996). School-wide professional community: Teachers' work, intellectual quality and commitment. In F. W. Newman & Associates (Eds.), *Authentic achievement: Restructuring schools for intellectual quality* (pp. 179–203). San Francisco: Jossey-Bass.

Macedo, S. (2000). *Diversity and distrust: Civic education in multicultural democracy.* Cambridge, MA: Harvard University Press.

Malen, B., Ogawa, R. T., & Kranz, J. (1990). Evidence says site-based management hindered by many factors. *School Administrator, 47*(2), 30–32, 53–56, 59.

Marks, H. M., & Louis, K. S. (1997). Does teacher empowerment affect the classroom? The implications of teacher empowerment for instructional practice and student academic performance. *Educational Evaluation and Policy Analysis, 19,* 245–275.

Martin, R. (2002). *The responsibility virus.* New York: Basic Books.

Meier, D. (2002). *In schools we trust: Creating communities of learning in an era of testing and standardization.* Boston: Beacon Press.

McAllister, D. J. (1995). Affect- and cognition-based trust as foundations for interpersonal cooperation in organizations. *Academy of Management Journal, 38,* 24–59.

McKnight, D. H., Cummings, L. L., & Chervany, N. L. (1998). Initial trust formation in new organizational relationships. *Academy of Management Review, 23,* 473–490.

Mintzberg, H. (1989). *Mintzberg on management.* New York: Free Press.

Mishra, A. K. (1996). Organizational responses to crisis: The centrality of trust. In R. Kramer & T. Tyler (Eds.), *Trust in organizations* (pp. 261–287). Thousand Oaks, CA: Sage.

Mullen, B., & Hu, L. (1989). Perceptions of ingroup and outgroup variability: A meta-analytic integration. *British Journal of Social Psychology, 29,* 11–28.

Organ, D. W. (1988). *Organizational citizenship behavior: The good soldier syndrome.* Lexington, MA: Lexington Books.

Organ, D. W. (1997). Organizational citizenship behavior: It's construct clean-up time. *Human Performance, 10,* 85–97.

Payne, R. K. (2001). *A framework for understanding poverty.* Highlands, TX: aha! Process.

Peterson, C., & Peterson, J. (1990). Fight or flight: Factors influencing children's and adults' decisions to avoid or confront conflict. *Journal of Genetic Psychology, 151*(4), 461–471.

Podsakoff, P. M., MacKenzie, S. B., Moorman, R. H., & Fetter, R. (1990). Transformational leader behaviors and their effects on followers' trust in leader, satisfaction, and organizational citizenship behaviors. *Leadership Quarterly*, *1*, 107–142.

Pounder, D. G. (1998). *Restructuring schools for collaboration: Promises and pitfalls*. Albany: State University of New York Press.

Putnam, R. D. (1993). The prosperous community: Social capital and public life. *The American Prospect*, *13*, 35–42.

Putnam, R. D. (2000). *Bowling alone: The collapse and revival of American community*. New York: Simon and Schuster.

Putnam, R. T., & Borko, H. (1997). Teacher learning: Implications of new views of cognition. In B. J. Biddle, T. L. Good, & I. F. Goodson (Eds.), *The international handbook of teachers and teaching* (pp. 1223–1296). Dordrecht, The Netherlands: Kluwer.

Reina, D., & Reina, M. (1999). *Trust and betrayal in the workplace*. San Francisco, CA: Berrett-Koehler Publishers.

Roberts, K. H., & O'Reilly, C. O. (1974). Failure in upward communication in organizations: Three possible culprits. *Academy of Management Review*, *17*, 205–215.

Robinson, S. L. (1996). Trust and breach of the psychological contract. *Administrative Science Quarterly*, *41*, 574–599.

Rosen, B., & Jerdee, T. H. (1977). Influence of subordinate characteristics on trust and use of participative decision strategies in a management simulation. *Journal of Applied Psychology*, *62*, 628–631.

Ross, J. A. (1992). Teacher efficacy and the effects of coaching on student achievement. *Canadian Journal of Education*, *17*(1), 51–65.

Rotter, J. B. (1967). A new scale for the measurement of interpersonal trust. *Journal of Personality*, *35*, 651–665.

Rotter, J. B. (1980). Interpersonal trust, trustworthiness, and gullibility. *American Psychologist*, *35*, 1–7.

Rousseau, D., Sitkin, S. B., Burt, R., & Camerer, C. (1998). Not so different after all: A cross-discipline view of trust. *Academy of Management Review*, *23*, 393–404.

Rubin, J. Z., Pruit, D. G., & Kim, T. (1994). *Social conflict: Escalation, stalemate, and settlement*. New York: McGraw-Hill.

Sampson, R., Raudenbush, S., & Felton, E. (1997). Neighborhoods and violent crime: A multilevel study of collective efficacy. *Science*, *277*, 918–924.

Sapienza, H. J., & Korsgaard, M. A. (1996). Managing investor relations: The impact of procedural justice in establishing and sustaining investor support. *Academy of Management Journal 39*, 544–574.

Sarason, S. (1982). *The culture of change and the problem of change* (2nd ed.). Boston: Allyn & Bacon.

Schein, E.H. (1992). *Organizational culture and leadership* (2nd ed.). San Francisco: Jossey-Bass.

Schlenker, B. R., Helm, B., & Tedeschi, J. T. (1973). The effects of personality and situational variables on behavioral trust. *Journal of Personality and Social Psychology, 25*, 419–427.

Shapiro, D. L., Sheppard, B. H., & Cheraskin, L. (1992). Business on a handshake. *Negotiation Journal, 8*, 365–378.

Shapiro, S. P. (1987). The social control of impersonal trust. *American Journal of Sociology, 93*, 623–658.

Shaw, R. B. (1997). *Trust in the balance: Building successful organizations on results, integrity and concern*. San Francisco: Jossey-Bass.

Short, P. M., & Greer, J. T. (1997). *Leadership in empowered schools: Themes from innovative efforts*. Columbus, OH: Merrill.

Simons, T. L. (1999). Behavioral integrity as a critical ingredient for transformational leadership. *Journal of Organizational Change, 12*, 89–104.

Sitkin, S. B. (1995). On the positive effect of legalization on trust. In R. J. Bies, R. J. Lewicki, & B. H. Sheppard (Eds.), *Research in negotiations in organizations* (Vol. 5, pp. 185–217). Greenwich, CT: JAI Press.

Sitkin, S. B., & Roth, N. L. (1993). Explaining the limited effectiveness of legalistic "remedies" for trust/distrust. *Organizational Science, 4*, 367–392.

Sitkin, S. B., & Stickel, D. (1996). The road to hell: The dynamics of distrust in an era of quality. In R. Kramer & T. Tyler (Eds.), *Trust in organizations* (pp. 196–215). Thousand Oaks, CA: Sage.

Smith, P. A., Hoy, W. K., & Sweetland, S. R. (2001). Organizational health of high schools and dimensions of faculty trust. *Journal of School Leadership, 12*, 135–150.

Smylie, M. A., & Hart, A. W. (1999). School leadership for teacher learning and change: A human and social capital perspective. In J. Murphy & K. S. Louis (Eds.), *Handbook of research on educational administration* (pp. 421–441). San Francisco: Jossey-Bass.

Solomon, R. C., & Flores, F. (2001). *Building trust in business, politics, relationships, and life*. New York:, Oxford University Press.

Spuck, D. W., & MacNeil, A. J. (1999, November). *Understanding trust relationships between principals and teachers*. Paper presented at the annual meeting of the University Council for Educational Administration, Minneapolis, MN.

Tarter, C. J., Bliss, J. R., & Hoy, W. K. (1989). School characteristics and faculty trust in secondary schools. *Educational Administration Quarterly, 25*, 294–308.

Tarter, C. J., Sabo, D., & Hoy, W. K. (1995). Middle school climate, faculty trust and effectiveness: A path analysis. *Journal of Research and Development in Education, 29*, 41–49.

Thomas, K. (1976). Conflict and conflict management. In M. D. Dunnette (Ed.), *Handbook of industrial and organizational psychology* (pp. 889–936). Chicago: Rand McNally.

Tjosvold, D. (1997). Conflict within interdependence: Its value for productivity and individuality. In C.K.W. De Dreu & E. Van de Vliert (Eds.), *Using conflict in organizations*. (pp. 23–37). Thousand Oaks, CA: Sage.

Tschannen-Moran, M. (2001). Collaboration and the need for trust. *Journal of Educational Administration, 39* (4), 308–331.

Tschannen-Moran, M. (2003). Fostering organizational citizenship: Transformational leadership and trust. In W. K. Hoy & C. G. Miskel, *Studies in leading and organizing schools* (pp. 157–179). Greenwich, CT: Information Age Publishing.

Tschannen-Moran, M., & Barr, M. (2004). Fostering student achievement: The relationship between collective teacher efficacy and student achievement. *Leadership and Policy in Schools*.

Tschannen-Moran, M., & Goddard, R. D. (2001, April). *Collective efficacy and trust: A multilevel analysis.* Paper presented at the annual meeting of the American Educational Research Association, Seattle, WA.

Tschannen-Moran, M., & Hoy, W. K. (1998). A conceptual and empirical analysis of trust in schools. *Journal of Educational Administration, 36*, 334–352.

Tschannen-Moran, M., & Hoy, W. K. (2000). A multidisciplinary analysis of the nature, meaning, and measurement of trust. *Review of Educational Research, 71*, 547–593.

Tschannen-Moran, M., Woolfolk Hoy, A., & Hoy, W. K. (1998). Teacher efficacy: Its meaning and measure. *Review of Educational Research, 68*, 202–248.

Tyack, D., & Cuban, L. (1995). *Tinkering toward utopia: A century of public school reform.* Cambridge, MA: Harvard University Press.

Tyler, T. R., & Degoey, P. (1996). Trust in organizational authorities: The influence of motive attributions on willingness to accept decisions. In R. Kramer & T. Tyler (Eds.), *Trust in organizations* (pp. 331–356). Thousand Oaks, CA: Sage.

Tyler, T., & Kramer, R. (1996). Whither trust? In R. Kramer & T. Tyler (Eds.), *Trust in organizations* (pp. 1–15). Thousand Oaks, CA: Sage.

Uline, C., Tschannen-Moran, M., & Perez, L. (2003). Constructive conflict: How controversy can contribute to school improvement. *Teachers College Record, 105*, 782–815.

Walker, K. (1999, November). *The foundations and the fragility of trust in school leadership*. Paper presented at the annual meeting of the University Council for Educational Administration, Minneapolis, MN.

Watson, M. (2003). *Learning to trust: Transforming difficult elementary classrooms through developmental discipline*. San Francisco: Jossey-Bass.

Whitener, E. M., Brodt, S. E., Korsgaard, M. A., & Werner, J. M. (1998). Managers as initiators of trust: An exchange relationship framework for understanding managerial trustworthy behavior. *Academy of Management Review, 23*, 513–530.

Wicks, A. C., Berman, S. L., & Jones, T. M. (1999). The structure of optimal trust: Moral and strategic implications. *Academy of Management Review, 24*, 99–116.

Wrightsman, L. S. (1966). Personality and attitudinal correlates of trusting and trustworthy behaviors in a two-person game. *Journal of Personality and Social Psychology, 4*, 328–332.

Zand, D. E. (1997). *The leadership triad: Knowledge, trust, and power*. New York: Oxford University Press.

Zucker, L. G. (1986). The production of trust: Institutional sources of economic structure, 1840–1920. In B. M. Staw & L. L. Cummings (Eds.), *Research in organizational behavior* (Vol. 8, pp. 55–111). Greenwich, CT: JAI Press.

About the Author

As a member of the faculty at the College of William and Mary in Williamsburg, Virginia, Megan Tschannen-Moran prepares prospective principals to be trustworthy school leaders. She uses a combination of cases, problem-based learning simulations, role playing, enactive experiences, and direct instruction to hone her students' leadership skills.

Tschannen-Moran's research interests center on the social psychology of schools and how the quality of interpersonal relationships affect the outcomes a school can achieve. Trust is central to these relationships. Tschannen-Moran has examined the relationships between trust and collaboration, organizational citizenship, leadership, conflict, and school climate. Another line of inquiry focuses on the self-efficacy beliefs of teachers and principals, as well as the collective efficacy beliefs within a school. In the course of her work she has developed a number of measures to capture important aspects of school functioning and the beliefs and perceptions of organizational participants. Her work has appeared in the *Review of Educational Research*, *Teachers College Record*, *Educational Administration Quarterly*, and the *Journal of Educational Administration*.

Index

OTHER BOOKS OF INTEREST

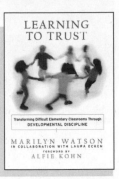

Learning to Trust

Transforming Difficult Elementary Classrooms
Through Developmental Discipline
Marilyn Watson, Laura Ecken
Cloth 352 pages / 2003
ISBN: 0-7879-6650-9

"In *Learning to Trust,* Watson's account of one inner-city teachers' experiences highlights the importance of nurturing caring and trusting relationships in the classroom. Her understanding of child development and her recommendations for effectively implementing 'developmental discipline' make the book a practical and powerful tool for all educators."

—James P. Comer, Maurice Falk Professor of Child Psychiatry,
Yale Child Study Center and associate dean, Yale School of Medicine

This book applies attachment theory to the school setting, showing how this perspective can help teachers build collaborative, trusting relationships even with their most challenging students. Watson describes the ups and downs of Ecken's classroom through the lens of attachment theory, while Ecken describes in vivid detail the ongoing life of her classroom, revealing throughout her challenges, thoughts, fears, failures and successes. Together they explore strategies for helping children develop the emotional skills needed to live harmonious and productive lives, the social and communication skills to be a friend and work collaboratively with classmates, the self confidence and curiosity to invest in learning, and the empathy to be caring and responsible young people.

MARILYN SHEEHAN WATSON has worked for more than two decades with teachers, teacher educators, and education researchers to effectively promote children's social, moral, and intellectual development. As program director of the Developmental Studies Center's award-winning school change effort, the Child Development Project, and as director of the center's national Teacher Education Project, she has been instrumental in defining education that has children's basic developmental needs at its heart.

LAURA ECKEN has shared sixteen thoughtful years with the elementary school children of Louisville, Kentucky. She is one of the teachers we never forget.

From Outrageous to Inspired
How to Build a Community of Leaders in Our Schools
David Hagstrom
Cloth / 208 pages
ISBN: 0-7879-7066-2

"Read this book with confidence that its author knows what he is talking about, and walks his talk as well. Here is no mere theory, but a model of integrity in leadership that can help us renew our schools, support our teachers, and serve our children well."
—Parker J. Palmer, author, *The Courage to Teach* and *Let Your Life Speak*

From *Outrageous to Inspired* challenges educators to think differently about the relationship of schools and communities. Instead of suggesting ways that school leaders might gain greater support from the nearby community, this book describes a school that, itself, became a community, including its parents and families.

From Outrageous to Inspired shows how all the people associated with any school—teachers, principal, parents, children, neighbors, and other community members—can take up leadership together to create a vibrant learning community. David Hagstrom promotes new ways of thinking about parental participation, neighborhood involvement, and teacher leadership in schools. In *From Outrageous to Inspired* he offers a guidebook for school leaders who are engaged in a journey of school improvement and community building. The book is filled with stories and reflections from Hagstrom's transformative experience as the principal of Denali Elementary School in Fairbanks, Alaska. As principal of the school he asked the question, "What do you want for your children, here at Denali?" These extraordinary stories offer a framework for creatively bringing about change from within an organization and for dealing with the larger issues of school change and reform.

DAVID HAGSTROM is a private consultant for teachers and principals. He recently retired as an associate professor at Lewis & Clark College in Portland, Oregon, where he taught in the department of educational administration. He facilitates Courage to Lead programs for school leaders.

Value-Added Leadership

Thomas J. Sergiovanni

Value-Added Leadership provides leaders with a clear and compelling way to help their schools achieve extraordinary results. In this book, Sergiovanni presents nine value-added dimensions which emphasize leadership over management, performance over participation, meaning over manipulation, purpose over planning, accountability over monitoring, intrinsic over extrinsic motivation, collegiality over congeniality, and passion over calculation. In addition, he explains how to employ these qualities through four critical stages of school improvement—from initiation to routinization. Sergiovanni also shows how value-added leadership can empower teachers, build community, and provide competitive advantage.

The principles of value-added leadership are as simple as they are powerful. They represent a set of ideas that have withstood the test of time despite the comings and goings of leadership fads. With this book, leaders have the tools to make their schools the best they can be.

THOMAS J. SERGIOVANNI is a Lillian Radford Professor of Education and Administration, senior fellow at the Center for Educational Leadership, and founder of the Trinity Principal's Center at Trinity University in San Antonio, Texas. He is the author of several books published by Jossey-Bass, including *Leadership for the Schoolhouse*, *Building Community in Schools*, and *Moral Leadership*.

ISBN 0-7879-6544-8   Cloth   192 Pages   2004

Ethical Leadership

Robert J. Starratt

In *Ethical Leadership*, Robert Starratt—one of the leading thinkers on the topic of ethics and education—shows educational leaders how to move beyond mere technical efficiency in the delivery and performance of learning. He challenges educators to become ethical leaders who understand the learning process as a profoundly moral activity that engages the full humanity of the school community.

ISBN 0-7879-6564-2   Paperback   160 Pages (approx.)   2004

Teacher Leadership

Ann Lieberman, Lynne Miller

Teacher Leadership is written for teachers who assume responsibility for educational success beyond their own classrooms by providing peer support, modeling good practice, or coordinating curriculum and instruction. This book explores the topic of teacher leadership by providing an overview of the field, a summary of research, examples of good practice, and guidelines for the future.

ISBN 0-7879-6245-7   Paperback   112 Pages (approx.)   2004

Distributive Leadership

James Spillane

"Distributive Leadership" is a new concept in education. It has to do with the ways in which leadership is exercised in everyday practice through communications and actions, and via others in the school community like teachers and parents. In this book, James Spillane, the leading expert on "Distributive Leadership," explores the distribution of leadership among various people in the school, and the extent and ways in which leadership is stretched over tools and physical materials in the organization such as memos, scheduling procedures, evaluation protocols, computer programs, and more.

ISBN 0-7879-6538-3   Paperback   128 Pages (approx.)   2005

INCLUSIVE LEADERSHIP   James Ryan
ISBN 0-7879-6508-1   Paperback   128 Pages (approx.)   2005

TURNAROUND LEADERSHIP   Michael Fullan
ISBN 0-7879-6985-0   Paperback   128 Pages (approx.)   2005

SUSTAINING LEADERSHIP   Andy Hargreaves, Dean Fink
ISBN 0-7879-7277-0   Paperback   128 Pages (approx.)   2005

LEARNER-CENTERED LEADERSHIP   Geoffrey Southworth
ISBN 0-7879-7553-2   Paperback   128 Pages (approx.)   2005